IN THE COMPANY OF
WILD
BEARS

IN THE COMPANY OF
WILD
BEARS

A Celebration of Backcountry
Grizzlies and Black Bears

Howard Smith

Photographs by
Michael H. Francis

THE LYONS PRESS
Guilford, Connecticut
AN IMPRINT OF THE GLOBE PEQUOT PRESS

The Lyons Press is an imprint of The Globe Pequot Press.

10 9 8 7 6 5 4 3 2 1

Printed in the United States of America

DESIGNED BY CLAIRE ZOGHB

Library of Congress Cataloging-in-Publication Data

Smith, Howard, 1949–
In the company of wild bears / Howard Smith ; photographs by Michael
H. Francis.
     p. cm.
     ISBN-13: 978-1-59228-952-3 (alk. paper)
     ISBN-10: 1-59228-952-5 (alk. paper)
Bears—Behavior—North America—Anecdotes.   2. Human-animal
relationships—
North America—Anecdotes. I. Title.
   QL737.C27S613 2006
   599.78—dc22
                       2006004686

H.S.:
For my favorite bear magnet, Valerie

M.F.:
I would like to dedicate this book to my
wonderful wife, Victoria, and to my daughters,
Elizabeth and Emily

TABLE OF
CONTENTS

ACKNOWLEDGMENTS

Over the decades, thousands of women and men have fought valiantly to protect bears and bear habitat. These volunteers, professionals, educators, activists, and everyday citizens have made it possible for the rest of us to enjoy bears. We owe them a large debt of gratitude for the contributions they make while laboring under taxing conditions, and for their success when the odds seem enormously against their progress.

Howard Smith would like to thank the many bears he has encountered for the gifts they have given to him and their good judgment in letting him walk away aglow with the spirit of wildness.

A special note of thanks is due to Kaleena Cote, assistant editor at The Lyons Press, who championed this book from its inception and who gently guided improvements. Thank you, Kaleena.

—Howard Smith, March 2006

It seems like bears have always been a part of my life. For this project I traveled from the tip of Maine to Florida and from the Northwest Territories of Canada to the Midwestern states including Minnesota. I put in most of my bear watching time in Montana, Wyoming, and Alaska. The bears of Alaska have an especially good friend in Charles Keim who has graciously guided me to his many favorite spots time and time again. I want to thank Howard Smith for his great text and I invite you, the reader, to enjoy the many places he and I call bear country!

—Michael H. Francis, March 2006

Welcome to bear country! All your senses go on alert when you run across a set of tracks like these.

FOREWORD

Welcome to IN THE COMPANY OF WILD BEARS. This book celebrates bears in photographs and backcountry tales. If you love bears, these stories and pictures will envelope you like a well-worn sweater. On the other hand, if you're somewhat afraid of bears, this book will help you see them from a kinder, gentler perspective. Many books published on bears (grizzlies in particular) purposefully cater to people's fears. This reinforces a widespread myth that bears are gruesomely dangerous, implying that they should be eradicated. Yet, the vast majority of people-bear run-ins are thrilling and inspirational encounters.

By the time you turn this book's last page, you will possess a renewed passion for bears or a new appreciation of them as something inherently precious and vital to our lives. The wellness of grizzly, Alaskan brown bear, and black bear populations acts as a barometer on the health of ecosystems, as well as on the quality of our lives. Through this book you will see the immeasurable value of maintaining ecosystems and systems of ecosystems able to support huge omnivores with requisite flora and fauna—verdant wildlife.

Readers should understand that they don't have to encounter grizzly bears or black bears in order to reap rich rewards. Simply knowing that bears could be present is enough to awaken our senses and give us insights that have long since died—dried up with urban life. There is substantial value in realizing that the great outdoors is, indeed, *wild*. Grasping this concept enables us to live life as we once lived it—vibrantly attuned to every second.

And now, come join us in walking in the company of wild bears.

Even though we think of bears as predators, which they are, the bulk of their food is vegetation.

INTRODUCTION

Bear.

What images come to mind when someone says this word or you see it in print? Are they positive thoughts, or negative? Do you primarily think about "large heavy mammals having long shaggy hair, rudimentary tail, and plantigrade feet and feeding largely on fruit and insects as well as on flesh"—the dictionary definition? Or, on the other hand, does an uncouth person come to mind, or perhaps someone who is unloading securities in the face of a down market? More likely than not, your thoughts turned to the former description—a powerful beast with the capacity to eat you or inflict serious damage. But why do we tend to associate physical harm with bears? As children we clutch teddy bears—an indelible icon of our youth. How do we flip-flop from lovingly embracing them, to avoiding bears at any cost?

A subadult male in the Yellowstone ecosystem is concentrating on filling his belly during the autumn months before hibernation.

Historically, people have vilified animals possessing the capacity to maul or kill them. Bears, wolves, and mountain lions are a few examples of large mammals that we have eradicated for our own safety, or that of our livestock. However, we reserve a special place in our hearts for bears, even though they have been relentlessly persecuted to the point of extinction in some locations. This illustrates our long-standing love-hate relationship with the Family Ursidae. We heartily laugh about their zany circus or zoo antics and give cuddly caricatures of them as presents. But all of this fondness evaporates the minute we set foot in wilderness or near-wilderness areas. Then bears morph into wild and perilous animals.

As a society we're mesmerized by the danger bears represent. They are out there, hungry and looking for an easy meal at any time of the day or night. Our media—nature and adventure shows on television, popular magazines, and newspapers—have done an excellent job of informing us about virtually every human-bear encounter resulting in serious injury or death. Bear maulings, especially those ending in someone's death, are front-page news. We nurture a macabre fascination for these adverse encounters. Such stories only reinforce the myth of bears as ferocious creatures obsessed with the intention of killing people.

Few stories explain how people often unthinkingly entice bears, resulting in harm to themselves or others. The culprit is almost always the bear—not the person. Some poor soul was innocently walking down a mountain path when, for no apparent reason, a bear jumped out and proceeded to flatten the intruder. Never mind that facts show the victim was pressing ever closer in order to get a better view or a world-class photo of the bear. There is a tendency to conveniently overlook the fact that a hiker failed to gradually back off after discovering the bear was feeding on a carcass. As a result, we form an image in our collective minds that any bear encounter will lead to overwhelming disaster.

Despite all of the extremely bad press, humans have positive run-ins with bears all the time without incurring the slightest injury. These uplifting stories never reach the pages of newspapers, outdoor adventure magazines, or nightly news broadcasts. We come away from these encounters breathless and charged through with amazement. Our lives are a bit more inspired due to the glorious opportunity to share a few moments with a truly wild and unpredictable animal—one capable of inflicting great bodily harm if it chooses to do so. Yet, to our amazement, they invariably walk off into the bush or across a stream, refusing to enter into any confrontation.

Mosquitoes and black flies in early summer in the north woods can be a pain for humans as well as bears.

IN THE COMPANY OF WILD BEARS is about the other side of the equation. If you are prudent about walking in the woods or through remote wilderness areas, bears will inspire your life. Even the mere hint of their presence enlivens adventurous journeys. People tend to step more carefully when they utilize the full array of their senses to remain alert. They don't assume that travel is 100 percent safe. As a result, they have the opportunity to be more observant; to walk cautiously around a blind corner or through a tangle of shrubs; to notice tracks in the dust or mud; or to question mysterious excavations alongside trails. Mornings are a little bit sweeter for having survived a night in a flimsy tent with only a thin film of nylon overhead as protection.

In many of our parks bears have learned to beg, steal, or otherwise gain access to unnatural foods. It is best to follow all rules to keep bears wild.

This book celebrates being in the company of bears—black bears (*Ursus americanus*), Alaskan brown bears (*Ursus arctos*), and grizzly bears (*Ursus arctos horribilis*)—as told in photographs and true-life encounters. The following stories are representative of what it means to walk in bear country. By doing the right things—such as walking quietly, starting early in the day, or following trails that provide access to water and food sources—you may be graced with bear encounters. Usually people stumble upon bears quite innocently, and these chance encounters offer the richest return. But even in calculated run-ins—such as visiting wilderness with high bear concentrations—the confrontations leave us gasping for breath and wanting to experience more.

People don't necessarily have to see bears to enjoy being in their company. For example, one morning after the previous night's raging thunderstorm, you may be hiking up a high canyon ravine and discover a fresh paw print in a puddle of mud. This should snap you to attention, possibly transforming a gentle walk in the woods into a thrilling expedition. In the same fashion, coming upon a screaming-red trail post sign in Glacier National Park that warns visitors about bears frequenting a trail can be positively electrifying. Pure adrenaline-pumping excitement infuses your hike even though bears may refuse to show themselves.

Bears are catalysts to living a big, rich life in the outdoors. It's not necessary to make visual contact. Knowing bears might be around is sufficient for us to walk more cautiously, to be on our guard, and to open our senses (and imaginations) to infinite possibilities.

As you read IN THE COMPANY OF WILD BEARS, it is absolutely essential to remember that people should exercise due diligence while in bear territory—but there's no need to be hysterical with fear. Don't avoid places where bears live, but *do* practice prudent outdoor craft to ensure a safe journey. Travel in small groups. Carry pepper spray. Make your presence known when vegetation closes in. If you suddenly encounter a bear, stop and slowly back off if possible. Don't run or you will resemble prey. Give the bear time to adjust. Remember that if charged, most bears are just bluffing. Play dead if touched by a grizzly. Fight back if touched by a black bear. Learn these and other rules of thumb for safety's sake.

Numerous books are available on how to survive in bear country, and you should read as many of them as you can. Learn about bear behavior so that you have a better idea about how they will react should you be lucky enough to stumble upon one. Supplement your knowledge with a proper can of bear spray—it could save your life. Above all, don't forget to keep a healthy sense of wonder about bears. Treat them with respect, just as you expect to be treated. And at the end of the day, be certain to share your fascinating and thrilling encounters with others so they, too, may understand the good that comes from being in the company of wild bears.

1

RETURN TO PRIMAL WAYS

Snap!

I hear a branch crack and time grinds to a halt. It's not quite 7:00 A.M.; early enough to be looking for wildlife, especially here, and in the middle of the week. Many animals seem to sense when legions of weekend warriors are back at their jobs leaving them free to roam. This increases the chance of running into wild critters unexpectedly. With that single snap my senses undergo a metamorphosis at the speed of light. I'm living totally in the present. What made that noise?

I'm hardly breathing, setting each foot down as softly as possible and scanning the east

Ravens are basically coyotes with wings. Like a coyote, there is nothing that goes on in their backyard that they are not aware of. Watch ravens for a while and they will lead you to other wildlife, such as wolves or bears.

side of the trail for movement. I'm straining so hard to listen that my gut feels like it's about to burst. A raven is caw-caw-cawing loudly to my right about one hundred feet above the trail, scolding whatever is ahead of me. It continues to harass something that it perceives to be threatening; something it deeply resents. But a quick scan of the thick forest reveals nothing.

Inevitably I begin to think about the parallels to walking in grizzly country. Any time I go down a path in country where grizzlies are known to abide, or for which there is sober reason to think they exist, my walk is always significantly different—better. It's akin to drinking Mountain Dew, having cold water poured over me—and being slapped sharply on the face—all at once. No longer on autopilot, I'm highly cognizant that I've unexpectedly become prey.

Friends think I'm crazy for being what they consider obsessed with bears. That's not quite fair. My thoughts aren't exclusively about running into bears; they aren't something that I worry about compulsively in the outdoors. In fact, I'm simply fascinated by bears—but certainly not fanatical. I don't have any headache-producing worries or fears about encountering bears. Au contraire; I relish chance meetings and the opportunity to watch them in action.

Admittedly, I wasn't always so blasé when out in the field. As a neophyte backpacker, the prospect of ending up as bear meat always occupied a little niche in the back of my mind. On solo campouts that corner of my mind exploded into enormous proportions, keeping me frightfully awake at night and ready to cut my way out of sleeping bag and tent should an attack become imminent. Endure enough of these sleepless nights and study up on the subject a bit, and eventually you realize the odds are pretty slim of even *seeing* a bear.

Finally, after a growing chain of innumerable nights tossing and turning until dawn, I realized that I had never even seen a bear in the wild—not one. I'd stepped around plenty of piles of scat, but could not confirm a single sighting of any bruin. Bear tracks in mud, yes; bear physically present, no. This was the moment that an entirely different perspective popped into my mind. I resolved to let go of those tension-filled hob-goblins whenever in the backcountry. It was time to relax and try to blend with the land rather than fighting it. Almost immediately upon making this one-eighty flip-flop in mindset, I began to bump into bears.

Before my attitude adjustment, bears may have been able to smell my apprehension and adrenaline. Now, I was striving to walk lightly on the land; to be one with the forest. Suddenly bears seemed to be coming out of the woodwork to greet me. I'll never forget my first encounter with a black bear innocently grazing on blueberries and wildflowers by the Golden Lakes on a western shoulder of Mount Rainier. Fifty yards lay between us, apparently enough of a safety margin that the bear continued to munch along nonchalantly. It all came together for me. Exercise caution, don't entice, be sensitive to what they may be feeling, and the experience could be pleasurable rather than painful.

Chance encounters began to accumulate, and with them, a growing appreciation for bears' intelligence, resilience, and resourcefulness. It seems like humans are trying to do everything possible to extermi-nate bears, and yet they con-tinue to survive. Bears soon became one more compelling dimension of why I enjoy wild lands.

My vision sweeps back to the left and I take two more soft steps before catching swift, hurried movements thirty-five feet away. My nostrils are filled with the tangy smell of

Bears have good eye sight, acute hearing, and their greatest asset is their sense of smell.

decaying aspen leaves from a late-spring blowdown, and a drilling sharp pine aroma from nearby spruce and fir, perforated like Swiss cheese from bark beetles. Without conscious prodding my nose is automatically sorting for a distinctive, unusual scent that might give me a clue regarding potential danger. I can actually *feel* the tangible presence of other life in the vicinity besides the raven and me.

A fumbling sound to my left immediately catches my attention and focuses my sight on a medium-size brown bear and a small black cub behind her. The very first thing that pops into my mind is the fact that they are scooting away from me, not toward me. Looks like I won't be frantically grabbing for some rocks or a stick to beat the sow off. Next, I stand absolutely still, not moving a single muscle. It isn't often that I have the opportunity to enjoy a mother and cub without fearing for my life. Several previous sow-with-cub encounters have been a little too close for comfort.

Both sow and cub look healthy enough. Their fur is bristling and almost glowing with the soft backlight of this morning's gentle dawn. What a contrast between the two, with the mother's brunette patina in counterpoint to the cub's eight-ball black. I'm also startled by how silently—

Every day is a learning experience for cubs. They have a lot to learn before mother sends them out on their own after two to three years.

though not noiselessly—they pad over the leaf-strewn terrain. If I tried to follow them it would be a pandemonium of snaps, crackles, and pops. How do they move so effortlessly and gracefully without making a sound?

They may have been feeding on the grass that flourishes down in the nearby ravine, where just a smidgen of water is trickling among aspen leaves. My untimely entry has them scurrying for safety, causing the youngster to fall after a hurried leap over a prostrate silver aspen that sticks up two feet and blocks its escape. The agitated sow has her ears pinned back—not a good sign—but she is on her way east toward the side gully. I'm not very crazy about her position between the cub and me. Seems like a good time to back off a step or two while I try to understand what she is attempting to communicate.

UNDERSTANDING BEAR LANGUAGE

Understanding bear language can be very confusing due to what people commonly see as unpredictability in bear behavior. Perhaps the best primer on this subject is offered by the Kodiak National Wildlife Refuge (www.kodiak.org/body_language.html). Bear language that is understandable by people can be classified as follows:

Lack of Concern
- Continuation with normal activities
- Maintaining a course of travel
- Continuation of fishing or other feeding
- Continuation of nursing cubs
- Continuation of resting

Nervousness or Curiosity
- Discontinuation or alteration of normal activities
- Moving off trail
- Breaking into a run
- Rearing on hind legs to look and smell
- Pacing and looking around

Moderate Agitation
- Woofing
- Walking stiff-legged
- Quartering away with lowered head
- Salivating
- Moaning or growling

Anger
- Popping jaws
- Salivating
- Bouncing on front legs
- Slapping brush or nearby objects
- Bluff charging

The trick is discerning subtle signs—ears laid back, yawning while looking away, or grazing as a means to ignore you as a potential threat—in what are often volatile situations.

Only experts who have years of watching and interacting with bears can be deemed proficient in bear language. However, even they have trouble distinguishing between a bluff charge and a real charge. Consequently, the safest approach for interacting with bears is to demonstrate respect through submissiveness.

There is another side to the story of communicating effectively with bears. The Get Bear Smart Society (www.bearsmart.com) argues that people may be more conversant with bears than they give themselves credit for, due to their interactions with dogs. If people can learn how to read what dogs want; they can also learn to read what bears want. However, fear tends to make people misconstrue what bears are communicating. The implication is to relax more and focus on what a bear is trying to say, rather than believe the bear is intent on eating you for dinner.

When in the company of wild bears, there is probably no more dangerous situation than encountering a sow with a cub, or cubs. Female bears are notorious for aggressively defending their young from any sort of threat. Studies by Dr. Stephen Herrero at the University of Calgary indicate that 74 percent of all sudden encounters with grizzlies are attributable to the presence of cubs. Bear mothers will do whatever is necessary to neutralize any threat to their young, including charging automobiles and large groups of people.

Black bear mothers typically send their young up a tree with an urgent woof or two. If this sow had stood her ground and woofed to her cub, then I wouldn't be standing here so complacently. I would be stepping backwards at an earnest, yet cautious pace, trying to put as much distance as I could between me and the cub. Running only triggers a predatory response in bears. So the key is to back up slowly, while talking softly, to communicate who I am and what my intentions are with respect to this chance encounter.

I swiftly retreat down trail, watching them meld into the forest, dry leaves foiling their attempt to depart as silently as ghosts. In seconds they disappear as though they were never here in the first place, but a sense of magic continues to shroud this vale like a comforting cloak.

My heart is pumping a mile a minute. I have violated one of the simplest rules about bear encounters—never get too close to a sow with a cub. After this close call, I'm totally ramped up and my senses remain fully attuned to the hillside above.

Cubs enjoy playing. Here a youngster climbs a small tree. Play is important for young animals as it keeps their muscles and reflexes sharp. Cubs have many predators, including male bears.

The raven is really dishing out abuse to whatever is traversing parallel to me as I walk up the trail. I'm looking, but not seeing. I'm listening, but not hearing. Only the scent of ponderosa pine wafts down from above. Fifty yards farther along after my encounter with sow and cub, whatever's above the trail is still watching me. Its piercing presence is as tangible as the black locust sapling at my side.

I swing around to the left—my back door. Where's the sow and cub? Have they dropped back down, ready for a little rumble? The raven continues squawking. What's going on here? Is it another cub that's stranded because I'm between it and the sow? Or, was a mountain lion stalking the cub? Am *I* now the preferred prey? Senses continue to run full bore. I'm ready to identify the danger and geared up to defend myself—but with what? A rock or a log? Packing light this morning, I had left the pepper spray at home.

There are no hard-and-fast rules about bear precautions. That's because bears themselves are unpredictable. At best, guidelines are available that suggest how to behave and what to use as protection around bears. The protection I carry depends on the type of bear country I'm visiting. If grizzly bears are *not* around, I tend to carry a can of pepper spray as a bear deterrent. The operative word here is *deterrent*. I consider bear spray to be a last resort that does not substitute for common sense, experience, and the responsibility I have to be informed by reading as much as I can about bears. That said, I have never had to use pepper spray to deter a bear.

Actually, I'm more concerned about encounters with mountain lions than I am bears. So, pepper spray in my pack does double duty. However, it is essential to remember that animal attacks usually occur in a split second without warning. Pepper spray carried in a pack will be more difficult to access than spray worn on a holster or attached to the outside of a pack.

If grizzly bears are known to be frequenting an area I'm visiting, then I also carry a little air horn. Available at sporting goods retailers and marine/yachting stores, I think these horns are very useful as animal deterrents because they emit piercingly outrageous sounds. One little blast and my ears hurt for a good half-hour or so. I don't think it would be any different for a bear or cougar. Like pepper spray, I have never had to use an air horn in the field.

In grizzly country all the deterrents are out of my pack and very accessible, if not in hand. Most unexpected bear encounters leave little more than two seconds for a response. That's why pepper spray purveyors also tout holsters as integral to their spray's effectiveness. I usually keep my spray and holster chest-high on a pack strap. Nonetheless, I will admit that there's a large measure of comfort in walking with spray in hand, ready for action when moving through dense vegetation where it's hard to detect a large mammal.

It could be argued that a person tends to hike differently when carrying pepper spray, an air horn, or even a gun. I don't doubt that this is true for many hikers, who feel emboldened by their armor. However, they fail to recognize that the deterrent capability of pepper spray or an air horn is merely hypothetical, and it's not an academic theory I'm particularly interested in testing. Maybe that's why my pepper spray stays in the pack until I reach grizzly country.

SHOULD YOU CARRY A GUN FOR PROTECTION?

"Why fool around with pepper spray or an air horn that *may not* deter a bear? Why not carry a gun? That'll stop 'em dead." So goes another line of thinking about traveling safely in bear country.

Carrying a gun as a bear deterrent has dubious value. Most encounters, whether with grizzlies or black bears, happen so fast that victims do not have time to pull out and shoot a gun. They seldom have the time necessary to quickly extricate a handgun from its holster, carefully aim, and fire before a bear is upon them. Those carrying rifles or shotguns also must cope with the sudden surprise of a furry freight train bearing down upon them. Only outdoor enthusiasts who are expertly adept with firearms can rely on them for safety.

For those who are not proficient with firearms (and even those who are), pepper spray is vastly superior as a protection device because it doesn't need to be carefully

Authorities recommend carrying pepper spray when hiking, camping, or hunting in bear country. Remember to keep the spray in a place where you can easily access it. Pepper spray won't do a bit of good if it is in your pack! Also keep track of the wind. If pepper spray blows back at you it may become incapacitating.

aimed. Canisters emit a conelike fog that often reaches to thirty feet, offering a high probability of hitting a bear where it counts most—in the eyes and snout. Even the sound of spray discharging can deter an aggressive bear. However, pepper spray isn't foolproof. A modest breeze may be sufficient to adversely impinge on the spray's effectiveness, and even disable the unfortunate user.

From a statistical perspective, the likelihood of being killed by a bear is very low, which further challenges the advisability of carrying a gun. Consider Alaska, which reportedly has the highest bear population of any state. According to the Alaska Department of Fish and Game, nineteen people in Alaska were killed by dogs from 1975 to 1985, while only twenty people have died from bear attacks over an eighty-five-year period, from 1900 to 1985. These statistics seem to confirm the relatively low probability of death from bear attacks.

The Alaska Division of Wildlife Conservation admonishes outdoor enthusiasts to carry a proper rifle or shotgun as a self-defense measure. A .300 Magnum rifle, or a twelve-gauge shotgun with rifled slugs, are recommended. However, the Division notes that even though firearms are allowed in state parks, they are illegal in national parks.

Firearm aficionados can point to situations where the noise from a gun has chased aggressive bears away, and, when noise from firing a gun failed as a deterrent, bears were shot to death. In the same vein, I had a friend who was fly-fishing on a small stream when he came around a copse of willow trees and confronted a black bear sow with a cub. The distance across this stream between him and these bears suddenly grew infinitesimal. The sow hammered the ground with her front paws and legs and took several steps forward.

My friend was carrying a large-caliber, snub-nosed handgun in a belly pouch around his waist. He dropped his rod and quickly pulled out the gun. One shot was all it took to dissuade her from coming closer. But, as my friend recollected, he was mighty glad he was packing iron given that sow's demeanor.

Ultimately there is no right or wrong answer about carrying firearms as a safety measure against bears. Used by experts in legal settings, guns can be extremely effective in bear attacks. For the rest of us, while guns may have value as a psychological crutch, pepper spray has a higher likelihood of being used proficiently, and with a successful outcome.

My intuitive sense of the trail this early morning urges me to keep going rather than turn back. As long as that raven is up there, flapping along and squawking away to its heart's content, I know exactly where the mystery life-form dwells. I cut back a bit on my hypervigilance and throw it all into a very quick walk—not a run, because it might be a mountain lion that waits up trail. In minutes, the wild raven and mystery guest are left behind. I hit a portion of trail that switchbacks rapidly, gaining one hundred feet, and the change in elevation feels much better. Now I'm slightly above the contour at which the ambiguous beast and raven last carried on their tête-à-tête.

And then, silence closes in again.

Even though I've run into bears galore, from gigantic to puny, aggressive to lethargic, this morning's wake-up call has ratcheted up my adrenaline level and attentiveness. It's no longer a casual walk up a trail that I've hiked two or three times a week; now there is a detectable difference. *It's a tangible return to primal ways.*

Inexplicably, I find myself concentrating like an overachieving student studying for finals. I ask myself, "What's the big deal?" I've had plenty of bear encounters, some much closer than this. I know what to look for and how to walk carefully in bear country to avoid becoming a statistic. My reactions have always been razor-sharp, and the right choices occurred quite naturally. Nonetheless, here I am intensely scanning the trail and surrounding terrain like I've never seen a bear before. I'm especially cognizant of the trailside cover and rocky ledges located above me, where a surreptitiously hidden bear could lunge downhill upon an unsuspecting target.

Senses ramp up with startling acuity; my vision is simultaneously focused and expansive. I've got the immediate vicinity completely covered, while every other second I glance ahead to take a security reading. My hearing attunes with unbelievable discernment. I'm able to shut out extraneous sounds, intent on hearing another unusual snap. My steps are lighter and more agile. Each footfall is merely preliminary while I'm coiled to spring into action without the slightest hesitation. It's not tentativeness, but a testing at every movement in case I've crossed over a bear's imagined safety boundary.

Contemplate walking like this all of the time, every second that you are on a trail or in camp. In ancient days this is pretty much how people always walked, if they wanted to live a long life. Our ancestors didn't know what or who was out there lurking around the next bend, waiting in ambush. They couldn't just put themselves on cruise control like we do today.

This return to primal ways—living with senses vibrantly raw—is boldly refreshing. I relish every calculated movement, each step and breath. *This is the essence of why I enjoy walking in the company of wild bears.*

MAKING ROOM FOR BEARS

Life lived fully in the present, in the moment—that's what distinguishes bear country and, in turn, justifies setting large tracts of land aside to make certain that bears don't wink out of existence. However, it isn't *just* about the health and welfare of bears. It's about every living organism and inanimate thing needed to keep them going. It's about access to pine nuts from white fir maturing at just the right time and in just the right amount. It's about millions of moths hatching under rocks in vast scree piles along the Continental Divide. Each nanobite of protein adds up in big ways, just as ripe berries add healthy layers of fat to see bears through hibernation.

To ensure that we have places for experiencing the thrill of living second to second, society must make some sacrifices. Bears and ecosystems needed to sustain them are scarce. Yet, people can't enjoy wildness without wilderness. To have wilderness we must have humongous acreage because that's what it takes to maintain populations of moose, deer, puma, wolves, and grizzly bears, and all of the other flora and fauna relying on mutual sustainability. Large ecosystems set aside in a few remote places won't fill the bill. We need systems of ecosystems allowing safe migration and healthy gene pools. In short, more wilderness is needed; more wildlands, and less incursion on that which exists.

As human populations burgeon, wildness evaporates and with it species that we can never reclaim. Things can never be the same once species are lost. They are gone forever. This is the urgent rationale for stopping unchecked growth. When we finally reach the point where we want what we've lost, it can never be returned to its original state. It's simply gone forever. So the time is now to set aside vast tracts of land.

It won't be getting any better unless we do something about it. Our society needs to make more progress in conserving land. We don't have to use these large tracts to appreciate their value; it's enough to know that they are there. Wallace Stegner captured this notion rather eloquently in *The Sound of Mountain Water*: "We simply need that wild country available to us, even if we never do more than to drive to its edge and look in." People don't have to use wilderness to give it value. The fact that it exists gives it inherent worth. Nurture large ecosystems. Make room for bears.

Above all I notice small things about this mountain that I've never noticed in decades of hiking—the abundance of boulders on a ridge; a generosity of ponderosa pine blending into fir in a ravine; fallen oak leaves from last fall rustling slightly in an almost nonexistent breeze; the steepness of the hillside that looms imposingly over this trail; and the early-morning sun's reflection—how its brightness tends to drown out details on the ridge's south-facing slope and intensifies shady areas (where bears may be lurking).

In addition to being cognizant of fine detail, I feel dazzlingly alive. It's as though I'm making my first hike after being cooped up indoors with a long illness. I'm roused out of civilized life's foggy stupor with its attendant comforts cast over me like a thick, heavy blanket. To be—it's a marvelous feeling.

Continuing for about fifteen minutes on full alert, I'm beginning to question whether the mystery life-form that was above me is actually still close by. My intensity level drops a bit but I'm still quite cautious. I'm also beginning to climb into a phenomenally rich bowl of gigantic spruce and ponderosa pines. This is mountain lion and bear terrain. Although I've run into bear up here before, I've only seen scat and scent-scrapings by lions. In the last month I've seen several healthy scat piles and a few tracks. That's enough to make me wary any time I set foot on this trail's upper reaches. It's uncharacteristically silent here on these northern slopes, and the atmosphere is truly wild.

Thud, clunk!

Rustle, crackle, crunch!

A branch falls sharply to the east hidden behind a screen of towering black-green spruce and car-size boulders wearing caps of gray lichen. Not again? I stop and quietly take a reading through senses that continue to work overtime. As exhilarating as this might be, when the adrenaline does wear off I'll be exhausted. I wait three, then four minutes or more. Nothing materializes. No odor, movement, or sound. It's as silent as a tomb, and hardly a breath of wind courses through this forest.

Maybe I was just hearing things. Continuing onward, scanning everything in sight, I'm chewing over two intriguing ideas. First, I've gone

In bear language it is impolite to stare. In fact a stare is a challenge! This female has her cubs hidden close by and will not tolerate a closer intrusion. At this point another bear (or a human) would be wise to look away and retreat slowly.

through several levels of attentiveness in the course of this hike, yet this is a trail that I've become accustomed to as a weekly tonic. Second, what flabbergasts my mind is how totally different I tend to walk in wilderness compared to the city. In the backcountry my senses really do come alive.

Even if I'm only taking a short hike on a nature trail, I undergo an immediate metamorphosis. I'm not me anymore. Without consciously thinking about it, old ways bubble to the surface. The safety of a civilized life is left at pavement's end and I adjust accordingly because that's the way we're all hardwired. This is a hugely important value derived from wilderness—these feelings and the healthy exercise of dormant abilities that are never lost.

Considerably more alert than when beginning this hike, I'm focused on climbing rapidly out of the heavily forested canyon with its beasts and mysteries. I've learned a lesson today: Don't court trouble by leaving the pepper spray at home simply to save a little weight. For now, there's nothing that can be done other than to stay tuned to the forest.

Approaching other hidden spots along this trail where I've run into bears before, I anticipate and slow down, senses rising to the occasion—testing, sifting, clarifying, and deciding. But the magic is all done for today. I instinctively know this, having run the gauntlet before. Gad, I feel alive. To enjoy those moments on the edge when nature rules and ancient skills bound out of tightly locked and hermetically sealed compartments deep within me; this is what it truly means to live in the moment—to return to primal ways.

A vibrantly new worldview emerges when your senses throw off their shackles. It's as if you're taken back to childhood and reexposed to a wonderful kaleidoscope of new things to see, think, smell, hear, touch, and taste. This is what walking through bear country is like. Instinctively you know it's different. You may not be able to quite put your finger on it, but failure to explain just doesn't matter. All that matters is your pulse rising up beyond its normally staid level and feeling your surroundings in a most unusual way. In fact, you may find it difficult to distinguish between where your senses end and your surroundings begin.

Perhaps more thrilling is the experience of living second by slowly unfolding second in anticipation of something that may challenge your hypothetical right of way. Bears are quite proficient at contesting our privilege of living longer than the seconds it takes to shred flesh, sever a critical artery, or traumatize precious organs. Turning from predator to prey, you're unquestionably living for the present—for each precious second—and almost totally unconcerned about anything as blasé as the future. Even if you are well armed and carry sufficient firepower to do a bear major harm, you will still find the hair on the back of your neck standing up, armpits drenched with nervous perspiration, and more than a touch of panic beginning to overwhelm your central nervous system. I've come to learn to expect the unexpected while walking in the company of wild bears.

2

WALKING WITH ALASKA'S GREAT BEAR

Screaming like a wailing banshee, our brilliant yellow Beaver floatplane struggles to purchase elevation over the pancake-flat, black-blue waters of Cook Inlet. Seconds earlier we taxied down Beluga Bay at Homer, Alaska, on a deathly still and frosty June morning. Today we will walk with the great bear—the Alaskan brown bear. These bears reach huge proportions due to an amazing abundance of food along coastal habitats. Supremely large males reach 1,400 to 1,500 pounds, and unusually huge females attain 700 to 800 pounds. While our group of seven intrepid bear watchers may not encounter any of these trophy monsters, there's almost no question that we will walk with some gigantic specimens.

Riding shotgun, the only thing in front of me is a whirling propeller and a vast aquamarine sky that's almost totally devoid of clouds. An Alaskan summer storm blew through yesterday with heavy, bruise-colored clouds and periodic downpours, leaving today totally cleansed but unclear about where temperatures will head. We've packed for just about any condition because once the plane lands and we're on the trail, there's no whimpering or turning back simply because of a little cold or wetness.

The flight consumes about ninety minutes in covering one hundred miles of vast ocean, but time whizzes by because there's so much stunning beauty to see. The Alaskan Range towers over bays and fjords. Many of the snow-covered peaks are active, or recently active, volcanoes. Symmetrical

Halo Bay in Katmai National Park is a favorite fly-in bear viewing area.

cones—Mount Spur, Mount Redoubt, Mount Iliamna, and Mount Augustine—dot the horizon and testify about raw land momentarily placid in the throes of creation. We're flabbergasted by the enormity of peaks, glaciers, snowfields, and the coastline of the Kenai Peninsula as the Beaver slowly gains altitude, seemingly one foot per minute. Forevermore the Alaskan Range and distant Aleutian Range will alter our perspectives about colossal landscape.

The Beaver is exerting extraordinary effort to travel a blazing eighty-five miles an hour—gobs of bluster and hurricane-force noise for little speed. We don't want to insult the pilot, Gary Porter, who treasures this plane, but we're impatient about today's main attraction. We'll land on a small bay over at Katmai National Park and Preserve and then walk along an estuary toward a vast sedge-filled plain where the great bears are feeding and breeding. Gary tells us that we will be up close and personal with the bruins if everything goes as planned, and if we don't do anything stupid.

Gary is adamant that we follow his instructions to the exact letter. A few days ago he escorted a small group of bear watchers to this same spot—only they didn't fare so well. According to Gary, a couple of men acted like cowboys and their rowdy behavior chased several bears off. Worse yet, at one point they refused to demonstrate submissive behaviors—sitting still and refraining from staring at the bears. This is the sort of recipe that can spell disaster. If one of the monster boars thinks people are challenging him, he may decide to take whatever steps—from a gentle mauling, to disfigurement, to dismemberment—he feels necessary to neutralize them.

Banking right, the tiny Beaver spins a tight circle as we search for a whale's waterspout spray that appeared just to the east. There's no long torpedo shape floating near the surface, just a continuous progression of almost imperceptible wave ripples. Perhaps the whale sounded and disappeared into the ocean's depth. It will be another good five minutes before it surfaces so we spin back on course, droning above the nearly placid bay.

One minute Mount Augustine, an island volcano rising four thousand feet above the sea, dominates our view, and the next we're startled to find the Katmai coast looming large out the windshield. It's difficult to take it all in, to comprehend this land given its huge scale and wildness. I don't know whether to concentrate on the endless glaciers and peaks or to scan the shoreline and estuaries. Gary says to focus on an approaching green crescent that looks like a Jack Nicklaus-inspired golf course fairway plunked down in the middle of savage coastline.

It has become quite popular with Alaskan visitors to fly into bear viewing areas for a couple of hours.

And then we see them.

Three huge brown humps graze below about fifty yards apart from each other. As we buzz high above to avoid any disturbance, the brown bears continue to feed resolutely; they pay absolutely no attention to us. Their snouts are buried deep within emerald-green grass, searching for tender shoots and yanking choice mouthfuls for their gustatory pleasure. Occasionally each bear's head rises to cop a quick look-see around before being stuffed back into verdant pasture. Only one bear bothers to look up at our plane as we skim overhead. Excitement meters peg as we realize it's only minutes before we're walking with them.

Gary eases back on the throttle and the great cacophony of engine roar lessens to something slightly quieter than a noisy motorboat. The Beaver slowly glides down as we turn over Cook Inlet away from a vast grassy plain where a good two dozen brown bears are grazing. It's almost comical to see these immense giants feeding like buffalo out in the sedge.

My mind is trying to cope with the realization that so many bears are congregated in one spot. I've seen photos of as many bears almost on top of each other at Brooks Falls and McNeil River here on the Katmai Peninsula, but I never dreamed that I would have this unbelievable opportunity. At Brooks Falls and McNeil River, the bears often sport white foam-flecked mouths, a sign of nervousness from proximity to other potentially lethal bears. In contrast, the brown bears beneath our wingtips show few physical signs of stress, perhaps due to the mile-plus width of this estuary meadow which enables them to spread out with room to spare. They are occasionally within ten yards of one another, often isolated as far as a quarter-mile distant.

In part bears are congregating here because of lush vegetation growing almost exponentially in Alaska's early-summer warmth. Rich soil on these flats coupled with virtually endless sunshine provokes wild growth among sedge grasses, and adds up to a bear's buffet fantasy. The other factor drawing them here is the prospect of romance — it is breeding season. For the most part they just mill around, feeding. But that doesn't prevent a female from sidling up to a boar and nudging him a little with her head or body, indicating her interest. More often it's the boars that are pestering sows, hounding along behind the females, close on their flanks.

It takes a special mother to successfully rear triplets. She has to be attentive at all times, especially at the salmon stream where males are known to kill and eat cubs. Notice how close the cubs stay to their mother; they have been trained well.

Our approach tightens and the bears swing out of view. Now, forty feet above the coast, we curve sharply, diving into a river melding with the sea. Then, it's twenty feet, ten feet, and finally, touchdown, as pontoons grab milky glacial snowmelt that throws up spray, splash, and frothing white waves, slowing our plane to a stop. We're home.

Exactly what is this fascination with brown bears? And why go to all the effort and expense to put ourselves in harm's way? These questions flash through my mind as Gary wades to shore and ties off the plane to a large clump of eight-foot-high fluorescent-green willows waving gently in the sun. Some might say that it's a little late to be asking these questions, but in many respects, it's perfect timing. While Gary finishes his work, we're forced to pause before literally leaping into the fray. Why are we purposefully seeking the razor's risky edge by confronting enormous carnivores on their home turf?

For me, much of the explanation may be traced to early wilderness adventures when traveling alone. It made sense to be intimately familiar with the largest predator out there. After several trail and camp run-ins with black bears and grizzlies, I moved from being concerned about my safety to being completely fascinated by these creatures. Imagine—bears can hibernate for six months or so, have their respiration and pulse slow to almost nothing, abstain from urinating or defecating, consume no water or food, and yet, despite all of these miracles, wake up six months later and go about their business as if it were no big deal. Add to this the wonder of conception, a delay in the embryo being planted in the uterine wall, and finally, the birth of tiny, sightless cubs. It's astounding, and almost incomprehensible.

A FEW INSIGHTS ON HIBERNATION

Alaskan brown bears hibernate throughout interminably long, dark winters as a means of coping with limited food supplies. Fat and fur are the factors that enable bears to remain in hibernation and to keep them from succumbing to winter's frigid temperatures. The length of hibernation—usually from two to seven months—is generally correlated with the availability of food. In temperate climates such as California and Florida, bears may not enter hibernation unless an extreme cold snap occurs. Black bears have been known to transition in and out of hibernation in warm climates, awakening and moving around a den site before returning to sleep.

Alaskan brown bears and grizzlies hibernate for longer periods, ostensibly because they dwell in colder climates. Unlike black bears that typically choose forest dens in logs, shallow caves, under tree roots, or in nests of brush, Alaskan brown bears excavate dens on mountainsides where snow provides a thick blanket of insulation. According to bear expert Stephen Herrero in *Bear Attacks: Their Causes and Avoidance*, the heartbeat of a grizzly drops from forty to fifty beats per minute, down to eight or ten beats. Their temperature drops from 98.6 degrees Fahrenheit down to 89.6 to 95 degrees Fahrenheit.

Bears do not eliminate bodily waste during hibernation. As their bodies create urea, it is funneled back into the creation of protein essential to maintaining organs and muscle tissue. This explains why they do not urinate. Bears also lose substantial weight during hibernation, with estimates ranging from 15 to 40 percent.

When provoked, their strength and ferocity is legendary. Here is a formidable predator that can kill us even when we're well armed and totally prepared. Consider the national park rangers and Alaska state troopers who flew into Kaflia Bay of Katmai National Park (just up the coast from us), where Timothy Treadwell and Amie Huguenard were killed by Alaskan brown bears on October 5, 2003. They cautiously approached the dirt-covered remains of Treadwell and Huguenard, knowing that a 1,000-pound bear was protecting the kill. Even knowing that the bear was there and would charge, they only managed to put eleven of nineteen shots into it.

Bears are opportunists. Here a dark colored young male grizzly bear is feeding in a recent burn area where vegetation is lush.

WHAT'S THE DIFFERENCE BETWEEN AN ALASKAN BROWN BEAR AND A GRIZZLY BEAR?

Brown bears in North America fall into the family Ursidae, genus Ursus, and species arctos. Two physical features are associated with brown bears—a concave or dish-shaped face and a large shoulder muscle mass or hump. However, many populations of brown bears have striking characteristics that are not shared by other brown bears. As a result, scientists have tried to classify bears into subspecies. This is where taxonomy—the scientific grouping or organization—of bears becomes very confusing. By 1918, C. H. Merriam reported over ninety subspecies of brown bear in the journal, *North American Fauna.*

Until the advent of DNA testing, scientists tended to agree on at least two major subspecies: Ursus arctos middendorffi (bears living on the Kodiak, Afognak, and Shuyak Islands in Southwestern Alaska) and Ursus arctos horribilis (all other brown bears). However, some authorities identified what they perceived as another key subspecies, Ursus arctos gyas, or the coastal brown bear that achieves great size due to a rich diet. These coastal bears have been commonly called Alaskan brown bears. Dr. Charles Jonkel in his book, *Bear Essentials,* indicates that there is interbreeding between coastal bears (Ursus arctos gyas) and other brown bears (e.g., Ursus arctos horribilis).

In a 1998 study of mitochondrial DNA of brown bear populations in North America reported in the journal Conservation Biology, Lisette Waits, Sandra Talbot, R. H. Ward, and G. F. Shields concluded that there are three phylogeographic groups (or clades) of brown bears: the Admiralty, Baranof, and Chichagof Islands of Southeastern Alaska clade; the Alaska, Eastern

Alaska, and Northern Canada clade; and the Southern Canada and lower forty-eight states clade. Scientific work continues using sophisticated genetic testing to understand brown bear taxonomy.

Due to the confusion among researchers and scientific data about bear taxonomy, *In the Company of Wild Bears* uses the terms brown bear and grizzly bear interchangeably. This is consistent with how bear experts Dr. Tom Smith and Dr. Steven Herrero classified brown bears in a study of bear-human conflicts in Alaska spanning the years 1900 to 2000 (http://www.absc.usgs.gov/research/brownbears/attacks/bear-human_conflicts.htm). Thus, coastal brown bears and inland brown bears are both considered grizzlies. Inland brown bears tend to be smaller and may be more aggressive due to constraints on their food supply. Coastal brown bears tend to be larger due to abundant food and a longer feeding season. These bears may have substantially different appearances, but for our purposes they are both termed grizzlies.

Grizzlies are able to survive in the toughest environmental conditions by being opportunistic. As much as 70 percent (and occasionally more) of their diet is vegetation consisting of various grasses, sedges, roots, berries, and bulbs, supplemented by small mammals, especially ground squirrels. Spring offers carrion along the coast and inland as well as a new crop of elk, moose, caribou, sheep, and goat calves. However, what sets coastal *Ursus arctos* apart from grizzlies in the Rocky Mountains and Coast Ranges is accessibility to enormous salmon runs in late summer and early fall. The absurdly rich diet of salmon enables coastal grizzlies to attain a size that is almost unthinkable further inland.

Indigenous people nurtured enlightened attitudes toward bears, treating them with great respect rather than fear. As I learned about grizzly bears and experienced them in the wild, my views changed accordingly. Most bear attacks seem to be from human provocation, whether intentional or not. Few reported cases of predation have been recorded. It's difficult to maintain speculative myths once the facts are objectively examined. Gradually I began to appreciate the bears, respecting their great flexibility, strength, intelligence, and willingness to tolerate all but the most incredibly stupid acts by humans.

Do we really need a reason for loving the great bear? Isn't fascination a sufficient explanation for why I was about to step off a floatplane and rummage around with these magnificent creatures for a few hours? Sometimes you don't need to have a reason for doing something other than the fact you just take immense pleasure in doing it. And sheer pleasure awaited as Gary dropped an anchor to secure our plane's drift in the estuary.

Waves lap gently on the pontoons and beat a soft cadence; quiet is immense after the little Beaver's buzzing roar. Looking straight down, we are only two steps from a narrow pontoon. The aluminum is wet, and a misstep wouldn't be too funny since our plane is floating in over two feet of water. Concentrating on the landing I walk a tightrope toward the pontoon's rear and then plop into the bay-cum-estuary. Gary tosses my bulging black daypack to me and I wade across the channel toward a thirty-foot sandy beach with a six-foot bank of willows and grasses.

It's sensory overload to the max as I gawk wildly around, trying to come to terms with the eerie silence and vastness of this land. First thing on my mind is the temperature; it's pleasantly warm with a ten-mile-an-hour breeze blowing toward the east. Perhaps in the high fifties, a virtually clear blue sky is unexpected. It would be pretty uncomfortable sitting all day in sleet, driving rain, a windchill reminiscent of winter's gales, or a sudden snow squall blown in from the Aleutian Mountains. If I've erred, I've erred in the right direction by bringing enough clothes to dress in layers.

A gray-white sandy shore stretches west for a half-mile toward the Pacific Ocean and east another three miles toward a precipitous rise up a rugged, willow-choked canyon. Bear tracks with distinctive claw marks well out in front of the pads wander along the beach. A cub's print—no bigger than my hand—mimics a mother's plate-size depressions. Another bear, a subadult judging by the imprint, strolled by in the opposite direction. The tide is almost at its lowest ebb; two feet from the bobbing water, their tracks indicate they ambled by an hour ago. Thus, we approach the bluff very cautiously because we can't see over the lip. Peeking over the edge, I scramble up the sandy dune and once on top find that the coast is clear. We nestle down for a quick bite to eat.

There's nervous conversation as our small group of bear watchers shares bear fantasies and conjures scenarios to test what Gary would do in various encounters, like rounding a copse of willows and coming face-to-face with a boar, or inadvertently stumbling onto a sow with cubs out on the sedge-grass plains. But it's all hypothetical until a monstrous hulk of fat, fur, and muscle waddles up to us. We're sitting here without so much as a gun (it is a national park, after all) or a can of bear spray.

This is truly wild and fascinating country. It is miles to anyplace where more than a handful of people reside. Don't be fooled by the bright-yellow Beaver rocking rhythmically in the hundred-foot-wide bay. That's no real security. Just the day before, Gary misjudged the tide and the Beaver ran aground—stuck for an unanticipated five hours in gooey mudflats that draw bears like bees to honey. They love clams and display amazing dexterity in flicking open diminutive shells with their long claws—hundreds of pounds of bear and only an ounce or so of clam. The bears always win, although they have to work hard in digging for these scrumptious morsels. Clams are a delicacy and the bears' powerful sense of smell guides them to treats hidden well below the surface.

Katmai National Park is so big, physically, that it defies understanding in much the same way that you cannot perceptually judge the magnitude of the Grand Canyon or Yosemite Valley. Across the estuary is a waterfall, but how wide is the river feeding it, and how big is the drop? We hear the water's fall pulsating in and out as wind buffets the tidal plain. It's over there. We can see it. But how does it compare to mountains, rivers, and willows back home? Like the Grand Canyon or Yosemite, we have to keep looking until our perceptual frame of reference reaches equilibrium.

Some people in our group are babbling like fools due to excessive anxiety and adrenaline. Perhaps their unease arises more from something they can't quite comprehend, a wilderness larger and more remote than they ever dreamed possible. When their nervousness is exhausted, we loll in the sun's strength and wind's caress. Then, it's time to go. After a half-mile along the rolling beach bluff, we'll drop down to sedge fields where bears are roughhousing, full of life.

Our first encounter is a fox den dug into the soft, sandy bluff. As long as the sedge runs green and rich, foxes have little to worry about from bears that are too busy eating and mating to expend energy on chasing them down. Forty feet away from the fox den and up a grassy hill is a colossal depression—a daybed excavated from the sandy terrain where a bear had been resting. The bed is obscure yet offers a great view toward the river and estuary plain. Its size is mind-boggling, something on order of a four-person hot tub.

The air is fresh, uncontaminated, and buoyant, with a tantalizing mix of salty spray and glacial crispness. An early brisk breeze has flattened. Now there's virtually no wind whatsoever, and warmth is beginning to build into a heat that's an infrequent visitor to this land, to this season. Towering mountain spires across the river call, but we're focused on our next step, that seven-foot-tall clump of willow screening the hill we're climbing. What's in the clump? Behind it? Stumbling into a bear now would be disastrous.

Continuing to weave around this undulating bench, it's unclear where we're headed since bear paths crisscross everywhere. We're following an almost indecipherable path due east, paralleling the bay-cum-estuary. No more than fifty yards after the clump of willows is another very faint path running perpendicular toward Cook Inlet and Shelikof Strait. The bears often head out to wave-battered shores in search of carrion that may have beached. Another thirty yards, and a more prominent path navigates between two willow clumps to the estuary's edge.

We pass up this side trail until seventy yards later, when a natural swale descends to the sprawling estuary plain. I'm totally absorbed with not falling down the swale's precipitous thirty-foot drop. On full alert with looming copses of willows shouldering us on each side, I'm certain that at any second a bear is going to come racing out and catch us off-guard.

Everyone seems to be on hyperalert. It's hard to take it all in at once because we're on perceptual overload.

Bingo!

Three medium-size males, subadults around 500-plus pounds, are hanging out together looking for mischief only fifty feet away from us. They wallow in several tepid mud bogs about the size of two human coffins. It's an interesting game they play: Two battle on hind legs, clawing and biting without any real aggressiveness or ferocity and nary a growl; pushing each other around in a tug-of-war, they demonstrate their dominance and courage. They don't get carried away with their play-fighting since they're just testing each other. Occasionally they sneak a glance upriver where a couple of huge boars are wrangling sows.

We're standing bunched behind Gary like a mother hen and her chicks. A few bear watchers begin taking rapid-fire snapshots with their cameras until Gary quietly whispers to look down and away from the bears. Ten seconds, thirty seconds, and then two minutes pass until he heads thirty yards east and softly tells us to sit down. We're no farther apart than we would be at a very large dinner table, still fearful of what's unfolding before our eyes.

We see the third bear— odd man out—submerge his face deep into the muddy waters and then loll around on his back. He does this repeatedly. Then suddenly, tag-you're-it, the wallowing bear becomes the opponent in a mock battle with the winner

A close approach at the salmon stream by another bear has these twin spring cubs alert and agitated. If the approach is considered a threat the mother will either take the cubs and retreat or will chase off the intruder.

while the loser crashes into the mud. When tired of mock-fighting, they graze for a bit, periodically glancing toward the big boars, busy strutting their stuff. Undoubtedly they've already been reprimanded by those higher on the pecking order. These subadults don't want to risk further retaliation.

Bear hierarchy systems are pretty straightforward. Cubs rank at the bottom, and large, aggressive males rank at the top. Dominance is all about being successful in combat—demonstrating the ability to fight off a competitor. Thus, twenty-pound cubs are no match for 1,300-pound males. Females are the exception. Although they are usually less dominant than males, when protecting cubs, sows exhibit extraordinary ferocity that even huge top-dog males find intimidating.

Far across the river four other bears graze peacefully in the sedge about a quarter-mile apart. Every so often these bears reach the willows' edge and disappear before replacements wander onto the playing field. It's all so orderly and calm. From where we sit—smack-dab in the open, but hugging the estuary bench—it's refreshing to know that these bears don't have a care in the world other than to stay out of the way of dominant boars and sows who have breeding on their mind; the perpetuation of the species. The only thing missing are cubs, but the sows know to keep their young away from hormone-crazed males who kill young bears simply to cause females to begin estrus.

BEAR ROMANCE

Once bears leave their hibernating dens and begin feeding, breeding will generally commence. Female grizzly bears, which tend to have cubs every three years, reach sexual maturity in their fifth or sixth year. Males reach sexual maturity earlier, but they typically lack the heft and combative ability to win mates. Sows look after their cubs over a two-year period, and chase them off during early spring of the third year in preparation for mating. Some males have figured out that by killing cubs, they can induce estrus in females. Of course, such a strategy comes at a high cost in view of the aggressive defensive abilities of highly motivated sows.

Bears will coexist during times of extraordinary food abundance, or when breeding. Since they prefer solitary lives, these times of social interaction are quite stressful, but necessary for perpetuation of the species. Older, larger, and stronger boars assert their dominance during the courtship periods. Dominance displays between males are common, as well as seriously aggressive fighting.

Once a sow's egg has been fertilized, it experiences delayed implantation. She will continue to forage and gain weight in preparation for future hibernation. When she is ready to den, the ovum implants in the uterus and the embryo begins developing. Gestation will terminate if the female is malnourished or otherwise not physically fit. In those cases, the fertilized egg is reabsorbed.

What's remarkable is the apparent failure of the great bears to register our presence, or at least, that's what it seems. In reality, they knew well in advance that we had arrived, not by sight but from their phenomenal sense of smell. Even without the wind blowing in their direction, they knew we were coming.

Deliberate nonthreatening behaviors on our part, conveyed back at base camp as inviolable rules to follow, are helping to maintain peace and order on the grizzly fields. Without these calculated actions adopted as a code among guides and visitors, the events might be a little more hot and heavy as far as we're concerned.

Two facts are paramount: First, when Alaskan brown bears have plenty of food, they're generally not thinking about human prey to supplement their diets. This doesn't mean that the bears aren't interested in us; in fact, it's just the opposite. They demonstrate an exquisite natural curiosity about their environment. Gary recounts the number of times bears have visited his plane, taking a bite out of a pontoon just to test it, to experience its fiber and taste. If something new lands in their immediate vicinity they will most likely go and check it out, cautiously, but methodically. And why shouldn't they? Other than larger bears, they have nothing to fear in a national park.

As spring is changing into summer, Katmai bears have plenty of the proper foods to eat. They are fundamentally vegetarians at this time of year, except for carcasses washed up from the sea. But they don't want to be patrolling the shoreline. For a few weeks each year, estuaries such as this draw bears to almost infinite food and the unusual socialization associated with mating. The food/breeding combination is hard to beat, and although they may be curious when they occasionally see people, they're not about to give up either the romance or the convenient all-you-can-eat cafeteria.

Second, these bears are highly intelligent. This is a vital fact to remember. They are at the top, the apex, of the food chain, and we are definitely below them. You might think you can outsmart them, but then you just might discover that they have a few aces up their furry sleeves as well. You don't want to test any false assumptions about their innate intelligence.

A favorite scratching rock.

They may look distracted and complacent as cattle; however, they are as capable of multitasking as some humans. It's just difficult to read it in their faces. Experts with dozens of years of experience only begin to attain an intimate working knowledge of subtle body language and posturing, but even they sometimes make mistakes.

According to Gary, the standard drill for a safe visit goes something like this: Visitors repeat the exact behavior every time; no exceptions. Consequently, as far as the bears are concerned, humans display nonaggressive, even submissive, behaviors. People walk slowly and they sit down when they stop. This indicates submissiveness. Humans do not stare when a bear is staring at them. This also indicates submissiveness. People walk and congregate in groups, suggesting that a confrontation would require taking on more than one human. People maintain a safe distance even though there are no physical barriers preventing them from coming closer to bears. This suggests humans have no interest in violating a bear's sense of space. There are no sudden moves or loud sounds. In short, humans—or whatever bears consider them to be—are entirely predictable.

Bear society is all about being bigger and more dominant than other bears. Subtle body posturing says it all. Simply read the posture and return the requisite demeanor or behavior. Failure to do so is a certain recipe for confrontation. Yet, even then, actual physical damage is limited so long as a lesser bear backs off quickly enough. These are the simple bear etiquette rules. Alaskan brown bears expect you to abide by these rules. Period.

Humans have shown willingness to follow these rules on the Katmai Peninsula, and when combined with the plentiful food supply, brown bears do not see people as a threat or part of their traditional food sources passed down from their mothers. Sure, bears are curious as can be about us, but they really cannot be bothered. There's just too much fun to be had, too much food, and almost enough romance.

We've been squatting for about thirty minutes watching this trio of bears. We know that at least eleven more bears are scattered a quarter-mile up the estuary, having flown over them on the way to landing. So we rise in unison and walk single file in close ranks toward this group. A taste of danger—no, adrenaline—lingers on my tongue, almost metallic in nature. A shrub-covered bluff juts out into the estuary and we can't see behind the hook of willows and dunes. Is a bear grazing just around the corner? We walk very slowly, not talking. The bears are closer, and then closer still.

We're not much more than fifty yards away from five grazing giants before we sit down. Two are clearly males—their humongous size gives them away. They are roughly 50 percent bigger than the females. At first glance it is hard to tell them apart, except for their size, because their coats are all uniformly a light, chocolate-tan color. However, once I view them for several minutes through binoculars, differentiating marks begin to surface: a torn ear; a spiderweb of scars on a male's snout; a short, light snout on a sow; or a patch of raw flesh the size of a Palm Pilot on the shoulder of another male.

All five bears are grazing, heads down and feigning ignorance of our presence. That's good news. Gary tells us they know perfectly well that we're here but they aren't even curious. In unison we plop down on damp grass, butts already soaked through from our previous stint watching the three subadults.

My hands are dripping from nervous perspiration. This is close—too close to tempt behemoths. We have no pepper spray, no gun. I wanted to walk with the great bears and now my wish has been fulfilled. It's a stunning moment. Senses are attenuated and I can see with incredible clarity, hear the rustling of every blade of grass, smell the fecund earth and musty odor of shaggy fur coats, taste the constantly blending ocean breeze and glacier-cooled air, and feel the sting of stomach acid as a magnificent boar grazes in our direction.

Every ten minutes or so a female approaches this bear (which we've affectionately dubbed "The Hulk") and subtly presents herself. The sow sidles over and, using her rear end, nudges the boar on his front shoulder. He acts as if he's disinterested. Boars at the top of the heap make the call. When they pretend to not care it is entirely their decision to ignore a lesser bear, or humans, and continue grazing. This piques the interest of another large boar that gradually drifts in her direction. At some indefinite point—indistinguishable to us, but not to The Hulk—he violates the perimeter of acceptance. The Hulk suddenly starts a swaggering cowboy walk, all stiff-legged, with his head swaying from one side to the other. The females quickly sidle away, leaving the smaller boar without any interference. The Hulk heads straight for the competition.

They're both standing on two legs with mouths stretched wide open, baring impressive teeth. The Hulk steps forward aggressively and locks his opponent in one massive paw while using the other to swipe at his rival's ears and snout. Roaring ferociously, the bears lock in combat, which turns out to be primarily all vocalization and little actual swatting. After buffeting each other for a while, the smaller boar—probably only 800 pounds—drops and crab-crawls away. Exposing his side, and turning his head to the side and down, sends the message of recognition that he's not top dog. It isn't enough for The Hulk, however. He charges toward the hapless loser and a short chase ensues. Fortunately, The Hulk chases the other boar toward the river rather than toward us.

It's an awesome display, and our nervous chatter dissipates tension. But, the show isn't over. The Hulk goes back to the females and couples

Two large mature male brown bears. These bears are trying to settle a dispute over a favorite spot on the salmon stream.

with a beauty that has a slight collar of lighter, almost cinnamon-colored fur. She's dwarfed by The Hulk and must be awfully uncomfortable in the hot sun with a nearly 1,000-pound fur blanket on top of her. But it isn't this pair that draws our attention; it's the smaller boar.

He swims out into the river to cool off. Watching him with field glasses, we see that he's just puttering along toward a flock of geese that has been floating and feeding in the estuary. All of a sudden he lunges at a goose, almost catching it off guard. With frantic, distressed honking, wings beating the bobbing water, and feet paddling like mad, all of the geese struggle to escape. It's a close call; too close for their comfort as they take flight. The bear rolls on his back and nonchalantly heads toward shore and out of our sight.

We discuss the event that just transpired. Since he had his butt whipped a minute ago, was he looking to take out his aggression on someone smaller? It certainly appeared that way. Or was it just a matter of opportunity—the geese just happened to be there as he cooled off? That doesn't seem like a logical explanation since he swam directly toward them. But a more significant question arises: Why didn't he come over and whip *our* butts instead? Was it just a matter of location and opportunity? Alas, we'll never know exactly what he was thinking, but we're all glad he was chased off to the north rather than toward us.

While these histrionics and guerrilla warfare are taking place, a very large sow is gradually grazing directly toward us. She's on a collision course. Each minute brings her closer—one hundred feet, eighty, then forty . . . We're sitting straight up at attention; no one is breathing. What's she up to? I look down to Gary who registers no alarm. At thirty-five feet, close enough to see flies buzzing around her light-chocolate muzzle buried deep in the sedge, Gary simply stands up. Nothing more. No vocalization. No waving of arms. He just stands up.

Almost imperceptibly, glacially slow, the sow begins changing direction. There's no quick movement, only continued grazing while her trajectory gradually shifts 90 degrees, and then 180 degrees. Perhaps she wasn't mindful of how close she was getting. More likely, she was a bit curious about who or what we are. In any event, a very simple change in our behavior, our posture, let her know that she was violating our space. Standing up sent a message that she needed to back off—that our aggression levels were rising. And, in the end she was just curious, not intent on mischief.

Gary explains that all you need to do is take one very sudden step, the first start of a desperate run, toward her. This would be extremely unpredictable behavior as far as the bears are concerned. It would seriously frighten *all* of them and they would probably vacate the estuary, pronto. A very sudden step is aggressive behavior they don't anticipate, and they would flee out of fear rather than challenge us. But it would also end bear watching for the day.

We lay back and relief washes over us, but there's more action out on the field. The smaller boar that was chased off has clambered back up the bluff. His nemesis is still coupled with the sow, so the coast is clear. How she is physically able to tolerate his mammoth flab isn't obvious. There's rapid mating action for several minutes and then the huge boar simply dozes off while still on top of her. Anytime she moves, he awakes, and it begins all over again.

Mating bears. Females will often line up to mate with larger dominant males in the population. Copulation may last for forty-five minutes.

The smaller boar scans the playing field and detects that his rival is all tied up for the moment. He steps up between two sows that amble over slowly and freely offer themselves. He rebuffs one and then mounts the other, having the last laugh on The Hulk. Frankly, I'm pretty amazed at all of this socializing and tolerant contact. It seems out of character with their reclusive nature. Grizzlies generally avoid the company of others except when there is abundant food and opportunity for breeding—exactly the conditions here at the Katmai Peninsula.

We're feeling pretty relaxed after watching bears cavort in the sun for an hour. Warmth deeply penetrates my black long-underwear top, and it's a struggle to stay awake. I chuckle to myself, remembering a story centered on Yellowstone Park that Tim Cahill shared in *Lost in My Own Backyard*. Cahill is frightened of bears despite having had numerous encounters over the years. His buddy talked him into sneaking up on a grizzly that was feasting over a bison carcass. The bear gorged itself for an hour and then rolled over on its back, fast asleep.

From his hidden position, Cahill could only see its wavering snout and hugely distended belly slowly rising and falling. Eventually the human began to imitate the bear. Having had virtually no sleep the night before due to nervous anxiety associated with this field trip, Cahill also fell fast asleep—only two hundred yards from this snoozing grizzly. No one in their right mind would ever fall asleep only yards away from an aggressive grizzly bear, even a sleeping one, intent on protecting its carcass—the sort of faux pas that could have easily led to a fatal attraction. Fortunately for Cahill he made it back alive.

Admiring this wild tableau, a tinge of realization rises that something's missing; after thinking about it for a while, I know exactly what's disconcerting. This isn't a wild encounter as I've experienced before with bears. It's contrived, almost fabricated. I sit back, chewing on this thought for a good bit: Imagine rounding a bend in Glacier National Park and finding a grizzly sow feeding on berries about twenty-five yards off the trail. *That* qualifies as a wild encounter. I didn't suspect she would be there—there

For brown bears the fall salmon runs come at a good time . . . just before winter hibernation. Bears gorge on salmon to the point that they may catch, eat select parts such as the tail, and then drop mutilated fish.

were no guarantees that I might even run into a grizzly bear. Admittedly, I didn't go to Glacier simply to view the mountains (although that's a good enough reason). I only knew there was a very remote possibility that I would see a grizzly. Lack of predictability made this a prophetically wild and very natural experience.

Alaskan brown bears wake from hibernation and flock to estuaries where there's excess food. They replenish themselves and linger while breeding before heading off upriver where salmon spawn. There's no guarantee that on any given day you can see a single bear, or thirty bears—but the probabilities are extremely high that brown bears will be down in those estuaries. If they aren't there, then salmon are spawning and you know exactly where to go to find them.

Instead of paying the price in terms of time and physical exertion to enjoy a wilderness experience, we use technology to circumvent the hard work. We capitalize on our knowledge of bear habits. What we're doing is scarcely different from hunters who use bait or salt to lure game. They sit in a stand high among the trees or in a blind hidden by high-tech camouflage, doctored up with branches, leaves, and brush, waiting for animals to follow their instincts toward irresistible lures. The manner in which we used Katmai National Park's sedge grass smacks a bit of manipulation. Is there really any difference between hunters who use bait to lure game and our use of sedge grasses as bait? Perhaps there is one important distinction: sedge grasses are part of the natural flora comprising this estuary.

We scheduled only one day to fly over to Katmai National Park because the probability was extremely high for seeing Alaskan brown bears. Gary knew where they would be because he had already been there several times that week, and the week before. If bears didn't appear where he anticipated, we had the advantage of being able to fly up and down the coast looking for congregations of bears feeding in similar estuaries. That's not a wild, unanticipated encounter. That's artificial. It doesn't make the bears any less real, dangerous, or fascinating. But it doesn't add up to a wilderness experience, either.

Somehow there's little consolation in the fact that the bay we roamed is pristine wilderness; literally a hundred lonely miles from anywhere. Floatplanes have made it less wild than it really is. That's hard to balance perceptually. There we sat on the fringe of the Aleutian Mountains with massive tracts of wilderness all around us, but the experience wasn't truly wild. Tonight we'd be back on the mainland, sipping good wine, eating a gourmet delight of salmon, and replaying the spectacle of grizzlies finishing their sedge meals and amorous adventures.

These weren't wild bears; they were habituated bears—habituated to human presence. They didn't run off when we appeared; they didn't come over and eat us; they were comfortable with our company. That's not *truly* wild. We have taught them to disregard us so that we can gaze on them like voyeurs. Admittedly, these bears are primarily interested in eating and mating so they overlook our presence as long as we don't come too close.

Even more damning was the realization that I had contributed to their habituation. By hiring Gary and his plane to transport us to the Katmai Peninsula, and by following the code of behaviors promoting safe bear watching, I had only added to the degradation of wildness. But there is another side of the story.

Floatplane operators and guides will expound on how they are aiding conservation and protection of the great bears. Guides point out that any contact is superficial at best. A tissue here or there, possibly a stray food wrapper, or at worst, a morsel of food, human urine that's washed away in the rain, human feces in some instances; these are the minimal impacts of ecotourism. Bears and people simply maintain a safe distance. If people violate this rule, they can expect punishment from the bears. Guides are especially vigilant, however, because they don't want to lose their livelihood, their permit to bring tourists over for bear viewing.

Guides view their services as educational. They're helping to educate the public about these magnificent beasts and building advocacy for conservation. An informed public is more likely to make intelligent decisions when considering environmental, ecological, and conservation issues.

A vibrant ecotourism industry in Alaska reinforces the rationale for protecting great swaths of wilderness. It's a matter of trading environmentally sensitive tourism jobs for ecologically devastating extraction jobs. Ecotourism is sustainable; logging and mineral extraction is non-sustainable. As the ecotourism industry grows, more voices are raised for protecting natural resources and remediating those resources that have been used for extractive purposes.

Guides will also point out that their presence and that of tourists' acts as a safeguard against poaching. Bear organs and body parts are highly valued in some cultures. Where there is a lucrative market, there are also unscrupulous entrepreneurs willing to capitalize on the opportunities. You only have to look across the pond to the Kamchatka Peninsula, where poaching pressures threaten the densest population of brown bears in the world.

POACHING FOR PROFIT

As with other illegal activities, there is considerable speculation regarding the actual volume of poaching bears for profit. In 2004, the Virginia Department of Game and Inland Fisheries along with the National Park Service set up a sting operation at the Dixie Emporium, a sporting

For many folks it's a once in a lifetime chance to view Alaskan bears in the wild from a close distance. This group flew by small aircraft to this remote salmon stream.

goods shop in Elkton, Virginia. Undercover agents purchased whole bears, organs, and other body parts before selling this contraband to traffickers. The shop was located several miles from Shenandoah National Park, a potentially fruitful reservoir of black bears for poachers.

In this sting operation more than one hundred individuals in seven states were charged with almost seven hundred felonies and misdemeanors. In excess of $61,000 in illegal sales of bear parts and ginseng were reported at the Dixie Emporium. This is believed to represent only a fraction of the illegal trade of bear and ginseng. It is also just a drop in the bucket of what is often characterized as a multimillion-dollar market for black bears. U.S. law enforcement projects annual poaching of black bears at 40,000 per year.

The World Wildlife Fund estimates that illegal trafficking of wild animals and plants amounts to $20 billion each year. Bear Watch, a Canadian-based conservation group, sets trade in illegal bear parts at $2 billion. These economics have resulted in decimated populations of Asian black bears and increased pressure on American black bear populations. Pacific Rim nations are high consumers of bear parts. This has encouraged the spread of poaching in Russia.

Bear paws are turned into soup ($60 per bowl in the U.S. and $1,000 overseas) or display items (such as ashtrays), while teeth and claws are used for jewelry. However, the most lucrative market involves gall bladders. In 2004 traffickers could receive as much as $3,000 per gall. After processing, bear gall is typically more expensive than cocaine. The gall contains tauroursodeoxycholic acid, which is used to treat liver disorders. Bear gall is a prevalent ingredient in Chinese medicine for treating ulcers, bleeding, fever, swelling, pain, and cancer, among other ailments.

Knowing these arguments, and having experienced walking with the great bears myself, I can't help but ask: Should this form of ecotourism stop? Too many people can spoil a good thing. Even one person can ruin a wilderness experience for another. We have placed limits in other wilderness settings; for example, permits are rationed to raft the Grand Canyon. Inevitably, we face the same prospect on the Katmai Peninsula.

It's time to head back to the floatplane. Gary wants to check in on the three young boars again, so we walk single file, a close-knit group, intent on getting nearer to the action this time. We're on a collision course when suddenly one of the young bears wallowing on his back in a mud bog sits up and takes notice. He's off his back and on his front paws, not quite on all fours. We stop dead still and turn our backs to him as though we're staring off in another direction.

An Alaskan brown bear uses an upright stance to better see approaching salmon.

Don't try this alone. We know that we've just aroused the keen attention of the top of the food chain, and there we are, staring off into space, wondering what's happening behind us. Only Gary is occasionally glancing around to see how the bear is reacting. We wait anxiously for his next plan of action.

"Sit down."

We do so with our backs to the three boars. I half expect my head to be ripped off at any second. All I can think about is how fast grizzly bears can run and how pugnacious subadults can be. Teenage brown bears are just as mischievous as teenagers of any species. If one of the young males decides to come pay a visit, he will be there in seconds. Only none of us will see him coming except for Gary.

By now we're getting into a relatively complacent groove due to faith in Gary's judgment. To tone down my instinctual flight response, I focus on grass poking up between my crossed legs. For a nanosecond my mind drifts in contemplation of seeing bits of white bone, a tatter of black fleece, and a shred of olive nylon fabric—by-products that remain after I've gone through one of the young males.

"It's okay to turn around now."

Again, by following the rules of submission and stopping just short of invading their personal sense of safe distance, we've fallen off the radar screen of these rambunctious teenagers. We hone in on the bears, fascinated by their playfulness and their carefree nature while a cool Alaskan breeze sweeps over us.

An hour later when we reach the floatplane, a salmon jumps, breaking the bay's tranquil surface. Circles radiate across the surface of the water. It's a sign of wildness; a single event foreshadowing a great migration. The spawn is just beginning.

Salmon are returning to the precise river in which they were born. After spending one or more years at sea, they return again to the stream where they were conceived. Only this time they have the responsibility of creating another cycle of life by mating before they die. All of this frenetic effort occurs in the course of a few weeks. Salmon flood the rivers, their numbers ensuring that some will escape outstretched paws and snouts laden with razor-sharp tools of destruction. Those lucky ones that make it by the brown bears procreate and launch another generation before wasting into death.

In a few days the brown bears will disappear up Katmai's rivers in pursuit of a salmon fest; until next year, they take their fascinating mysteries with them, leaving us astonished and flush with adventure.

3 ᘯ

BAILEY'S BODACIOUS TETON ADVENTURE

In the September 23, 2004, issue of the *Casper Star-Tribune*, environmental reporter Whitney Royster recounts the mauling of sixty-six-year-old Wally Cash near Grand Teton National Park:

> *Cash was hunting near Kitty Mountain and Pilgrim Creek outside Moran Tuesday morning. He was trying to "push out" a bull elk from a stand of dark timber at about 9:30* A.M. . . . *Cash came up over a small rise, and on the other side was the grizzly . . . "I knew I had to get on my face right away," he said. "She bit a hole in my skull, about the size of a quarter." The gash is above Cash's ear, and the grizzly bit through bone but did not "get into the brain," he said. "I heard her come at me again," he said. This time the bear "tromped" on him but didn't cause any more serious injuries. Cash said he had seen many bears during his few days in the area.*

For those who read this story in the *Casper Star-Tribune*, on one of the wire services, or over the Internet, it simply appeared to be another tragic tale of what happens every fall. Hunters wander the remote backcountry looking for elk or other game, and invariably, some stumble upon grizzly bears. If the unwitting hunters are lucky, bears slap them around a bit or maul them sufficiently to require invasive medical attention. The unlucky die despite the fact that their errors were unintentional.

What sets Royster's article apart from all the others is the location—Pilgrim Creek outside Moran, Wyoming, and Grand Teton National Park.

Flash back some two weeks earlier: Sparkling sun is rising on a new day over Pilgrim Creek in the Teton Wilderness as summer slips into fall. It's a milestone day as Bailey prepares for her wild Teton adventure; a backcountry day filled with magic and heaping platefuls of extraordinary luck.

She hardly stands twelve inches high at her shoulders so you wouldn't guess that Bailey is much of a trail dog. She really has no right to be out on the trail anyway. This West Highland white terrier was bred for show, not the dust, muck, weeds, gravel, rocks, and streams that trail dogs typically negotiate with ease. But there's just one little problem: No one ever told Bailey that she isn't cut out to be a trail dog—that she really should just stay home and enjoy all the pampering a princess of her lineage and bearing deserves.

You've got to be kidding, you're probably thinking. *How can any dog that small be much of a trail companion?* After all, you know what a *true* trail dog is—one of those Australian shepherds, border collies, Shelties, Labrador retrievers, or plain-and-simple mutts that can take the punishment of long miles, coyote encounters, high heat, and no water. A *real* trail dog could eat that little dog for lunch.

I have to admit that my thoughts were entirely the same as yours when my wife, Valerie, mentioned that we would be flying to Dallas to check out a new litter of Westie puppies. *Man, if you're going to get a dog, at least buy a proper dog,* I thought over my third glass of wine. *Oh well, it won't be my responsibility. And, there's always the canine kennel down the street. This dog will log a lot of time down there. Not my problem.* So went my musings after that third glass, and as I weighed the advantages of another. The bottle was getting awfully light and so was my head. *A Westie? Get real.*

Our flight to Dallas seemed weeks away, but before I knew it, there I was, trying to negotiate streets in a suburban maze. I couldn't wait to see what these people were like. *Who in their right mind would perpetuate this species?* And then the door opened and the breeder took us around back to her kennel. She peppered us with all sorts of very personal questions, and it dawned on me that it was *she* who was doing the interviewing, not vice versa. "What do you do? What type of house do you have? Have you ever owned dogs before—Westies?" So the interrogation went.

Meanwhile, three small balls of white cotton and a larger courageous lump of fur scattered across the backyard grass. They would play with each other—biting, nipping, gumming, mouthing, rolling, and pushing—before periodically descending individually and en masse upon the poor mother. They were so full of energy; more than the Energizer Bunny. But our eyes were drawn to the female, our intended puppy. She was smaller than the rest, but she gave no ground without first dishing up some major abuse to her bigger brothers.

We must have passed the screening test because one week later, I wrote a second check for $1,000 and sent it off to the breeder. Bailey, the little girl, would be ready for pickup in three weeks. My wife made an airline reservation with the plan of meeting the breeder and Bailey at the airport and then immediately turning around to fly home. Me? I planned on going hiking.

For weeks thereafter I was regaled with all sorts of useless propaganda. Her father was Grand Champion of this and that. See? Here's a copy of *The Essential West Highland White Terrier* and there he is on the cover. *Big deal*, I thought. *How's a runt like that going to take to the trail?* Vivid recollections of Christopher Guest's all-time classic movie, *Best in Show*, flitted through my mind and I snickered, thinking vile thoughts about actually attending a dog show.

Well, one week led into another, and shortly, there it was, a perfectly tranquil winter day. Time for a good five-mile slog, 1,500 feet up, to a snow-free promontory before scuttling back down to dinner. Should I take Bailey? Why not? Time to put this puppy to the test.

And to the test she went willingly.

Long story short, Bailey showed no evidence of her royal breeding. She just went hard, 100 percent of the time; scratching, clawing, and fighting her way up steep hillsides, playing with abandon on the snowy northern slopes. She did wild runs on reaching the snow, butt dragging with each swooping turn, bound for frantic darts between my legs.

By the time we reached the car, that puppy was plumb worn out. I couldn't help thinking that maybe, just maybe, there was hope for her after all.

Fast-forward two years. Bailey is edging into adulthood. As predicted, she can't keep up with my long stride nor can she take high heat or death marches. Bailey comes along on shorter hikes and watches wistfully when I go to the door with a pack slung over my shoulder, telling her to be a good dog. She knows where I'm going and does her best to let me know that she's none too happy about it. She really knows how to push the guilt button.

For many people there's nothing worse than a precocious, "cute" little dog, and that certainly captures my sentiments as well. Those who first run into Bailey see her as just that. I hear it all the time. Her pleasant disposition only reinforces this reaction because Bailey just seems to love everyone, slobbering them with kisses if she gets a chance. But my gaze goes much deeper than the furry white coat, big head, black nose, and pink little tongue. I know her true character; the dog I've seen on the trail. This pooch is bursting with try. She has a heart as big as a buffalo and it never occurs to her that size is any sort of a meaningful challenge. I like that in a dog; a heart full of try.

This past fall Bailey decided to visit the Grand Tetons and Yellowstone. Dogs aren't allowed on trails in national parks because as far as the Park Service is concerned, pets should just stay home. Pulling together maps of the surrounding national forests, Valerie and I contemplated the itinerary. A high point would be searching for wolves around the Slough Creek area of northeast Yellowstone. Bailey could stay in the car while we and other fanatics scanned for wolves each morning in freezing early-fall temperatures. The rest of the time we would hike trails in the surrounding Teton Wilderness, and that, my friend, is where Bailey's bodacious adventure began.

An almost perfect morning bloomed with surprisingly intense sunshine flooding the emaciated lodgepole pine forest around Colter Bay on the shores of Lake Jackson. Last night's crisp air rapidly began to lose its biting sting as sun penetrated crevices and cracks in the woods. The Grand Tetons were waking up aglow in soft gold, now transforming into brilliant yellow. Fall was definitely here—you could tell by the slant of sun and shadow, by a slight haze in the air, and by the chill's reluctance to depart even as solar radiation gained intensity.

The target for today is Pilgrim Creek, flowing out of high country deep within the Greater Yellowstone Ecosystem southwest of Two Ocean Plateau. One drainage over from Pilgrim Creek, Pacific Creek also winds its way to the southwest. Two Ocean Creek draining off the Plateau splits at Two Ocean Pass, sending Pacific Creek and Atlantic Creek to their

The Teton Mountains are home to both grizzlies and black bears.

respective oceans. Walk far enough up Pilgrim Creek, continue on various ridges, and you eventually reach Two Ocean Plateau, the area surrounding the Thorofare. This is reputedly the most remote wilderness in the lower forty-eight states. Legendary mountain man John Colter named the Thorofare for its expansive meadows that made travel in this otherwise difficult country a pure joy.

Pilgrim Creek Trailhead is exactly on the border of the Teton Wilderness. This is the second-largest wilderness in Wyoming at almost 600,000 acres. The Teton Wilderness also borders the Washakie Wilderness and Yellowstone National Park, making this an unbelievably impressive ecosystem. Pilgrim Creek runs through country ranging from 7,000 to almost 10,000 feet elevation. Further east the plateaus and ridges fall in the 8,000 to 12,000 feet range.

A three-mile dirt road cuts off Grand Teton National Park's main road to Teton Wilderness's border. By the time Valerie, Bailey, and I reach the trailhead at 7,000 feet, a sense of remoteness settles in. Only a few anglers and wildlife observers venture off the park's paved path. There are no grand sights or geothermal features to draw spectators, which further adds to the sense of isolation. A busted-up horse trailer squats in the parking lot, but there are absolutely no cars or trucks. That's a pretty promising start.

Sparse stands of cottonwoods and willows, dotting the half-mile-wide alluvial plain of Pilgrim Creek, are just beginning to show color. A few have bright mustard-yellow leaves surrounding them like glowing halos. Standing motionless in the still morning air, their days are definitely numbered. September can deliver some of the most impressively massive snowstorms that Yellowstone and the Tetons experience. It's almost as though the trees know exactly what's coming.

Their alluring color masks another reality out there on the alluvial plain. Now that streams have reached their lowest ebb, you can better appreciate the incredible scale of frothing water coursing off these mountains in springtime. The Teton Wilderness is nothing but a big sponge that soaks up snow all winter long only to dump it in great crescendos during springtime. The half-mile-wide plain testifies to powerful runoff earlier in the year. In autumn it isn't much more than a bunch of stark white

An alert grizzly bear in the Yellowstone Ecosystem. Notice that he is playing with the leg bone of an elk or bison.

sand, gravel, and rock bars baking in the sun. A few of the hardiest cottonwoods manage to keep their purchase, but judging by the size of the trees it's a pretty precarious proposition.

Pilgrim Creek and East Pilgrim Creek join forces across from the trailhead. To some they are probably nothing more than two nondescript streams hardly worth taking notice of, each little more than a spritz imprisoned among channels of oblong river boulders. To me these are wild rivers. You can see it in their clarity and leap. They may be diminished now, but they are always one good storm away from raging. Down here on the plain they are almost tame. But make no mistake about it; these streams have wandered through a most dramatic wilderness.

They've flowed past phenomenal rock formations, through expansive meadows, and along dense fir forests. Moose and beaver have called these waters home, sharing their abundant fisheries with otters. They've known cougars cautiously kneeling for a sip and bears lumbering across them. Elk and bison have sauntered in their riffles seeking grassy banks and safety from predators such as coyotes, which have been unglamorously dethroned by wolves. Yes, these are truly wild waters.

This salmon's quest to spawn after swimming upstream has come to an end.

The National Park gravel road is gated, but twenty-five yards beyond its barrier a screen of five-foot-high yellow-green willows masks where the stony road shifts into a U-shaped trail after crossing Pilgrim Creek. Here's where National Park blends to National Forest Wilderness, and trail dogs can roam free without fear of incarceration or financial penalty. This simple transition, this beckoning wilderness, is what Bailey's been searching for out the car window. At long last the car doors fling open and it's black nose to dusty ground, taking full measure of who and what has gone before, the residue of what's wild and what isn't.

With rapid cuts and courses Bailey quarters around the parking lot before heading up trail. She's taking it all in while we get our act together. Some scents are more pungent, more interesting to linger on before canvassing the area. And, by the time we're ready, she pretty much knows the lay of the land and what has tramped through here in recent days.

First obstacle is crossing Pilgrim Creek; hardly a promising sign that you are almost immediately forced to ford its rushing waters. Fortunately this isn't higher up in some canyon where rock walls pinch the stream together, making crossing difficult. Instead, Pilgrim Creek's bed is a most magnificent rock base with yellowish-gold brown stones and very little algae over which the pure, tinged slightly with green, Pilgrim Creek flows. Several substantial boulders add character and cause waves, riffles, and frothing.

Initially Valerie and I are reluctant to cross because it's deep enough to swamp our boots—perhaps two feet in the deepest spots. Bailey also pauses. Unless she makes a good decision, she's going for a swim, and she definitely doesn't want that if she can avoid it. It's simply a matter of taking the plunge; we're off for adventure!

Across the stream Bailey begins canvassing the trail ahead. She's quartering and keeping close until she has a better feeling for what the trail is like and what surprises might lurk around the willow-infested corners. Pilgrim Creek's wide-open alluvial plain is rapidly narrowing as we head up a canyon flanked to the west by the 8,274-foot-high Pilgrim Mountain. As pine, fir, cottonwood, and willow hover close by, forming an almost impenetrable corridor of vegetation, my attention meter shifts from enjoying a beautiful morning to being somewhat alert.

Valerie and I are each carrying bear spray, either in a pack's web pocket or secured to a shoulder strap. This is, after all, moose and grizzly bear country. I also carry a small but extremely powerful air horn as backup. Found at a yachting store, this may be our best defense from any animal attacks. The horn emits a piercing, high-octave blast that literally stings one's ears. It took my ears almost a half-hour to recover after one small screeching blast during a test run back home. It should have a very startling effect on wildlife that inadvertently crosses our path with the intent of confrontation—moose, elk, or bears . . .

Bailey courses up trail before dropping back, herding us forward. The path is quite damp in the black shade of lodgepole pine, fir, and cottonwood. A storm dropped rain and sleet four days ago and the ground is still saturated in spots hidden from sun. This provides an excellent medium for animal tracks, and I'm trying to read what traveled through here recently. Almost no boot tracks litter the trail, only hoof marks from packers' horses . . .

Hoooold up.

We're no more than seventy-five yards up the trail in a densely shaded grove of pine and fir when we stop dead still. Three very distinct grizzly bear

paw prints—two rear feet and one front paw track—are interspersed among the hoof traffic. Telltale depressions from imposing claws (claw marks twice as long as toe pads), toes close together, and minimal toe arcs (less arced around the palm pad) help to differentiate these tracks from black bear. Bailey comes over to check it out, but she merely feigns interest. She probably already knows the bear passed through this way and that's why she's coursing back and forth.

Seeing a grizzly in the wild really is quite rare. However, running into bear sign and knowing you are sharing the woods with such an animal is equally exciting!

The tracks don't indicate a large bear, certainly nothing like we've seen up in Alaska, but they do confirm that they're here. Judging by the freshness of the indentations and lack of erosion around the pads' edges, this bear came by in the last twenty-four hours. Tracks from horses, and apparently at least one mule, are blending back into the earth and not as fresh. These traces have such clarity it's like reading the morning paper.

If I had been alert before, I ramp up another whole level of magnitude. It's as though I've been dormant my whole life. Just a few paw prints and I can smell everything with such clarity—the musty odor of decay from cottonwood leaves, sun-baked pine wafting in from east of this copse of trees, stale perspiration from my long-sleeved shirt worn too many days on this trip, barnyard scent of horses past, and an almost undistinguishable smell of—grizzly?

I taste the freshness of fall on my tongue intermixed with a slight edge of fear. Instincts have me rapidly scanning the surrounding vegetation from one side to the next, lingering for penetrating glances up trail. It's as though someone took high-quality earmuffs off as I can now hear with so much more sensitivity. No sound escapes me—not a branch breaking across the stream, three leaves hitting the ground behind us, Bailey's eager panting, a sudden *whoosh* as a big raptor sails overhead, or a slight increase in Pilgrim Creek's flow.

Already my hand has reached the upper pocket of my shirt, fumbling to finger the air horn; I didn't even consciously make the move. Scanning complete, I drop back a notch in attentiveness, narrowing my field of view. I'm not frightened or even particularly anxious, just alert. Ready. Bailey also seems more attuned to the forest and its mood. Her ears are perked forward, swiveling, listening. The sensitive black snout is lifted ever so slightly; testing for . . . ?

We prod her up the trail and soon she's swinging back and forth searching for scent as we come to a sunny opening and signage pointing the other way, explaining that you are entering Grand Teton National Park. Coolness is evaporating as the morning slides past midpoint. After a few seconds we continue, glad for the reprieve of claustrophobia and ready for sunshine, air, space, and no blind corners or obscuring stands of vegetation.

There is no doubt when you see the hump of muscle above the shoulders that you are seeing a grizzly bear.

We're just beginning to enter true trail as we pass a large packer's camp replete with three grimy gray-white tents and a pen of mules and horses. This explains the horse trailer back at the trailhead and the plethora of horse droppings along the way. It's a pretty depressing site huddled amongst towering trees and suffering from a deficit of sun. A man walks over to Pilgrim Creek blissfully unaware of our presence, bucket in hand, and begins washing his hair. We pass unnoticed.

After the camp, Pilgrim Creek Trail really closes in and almost disappears in willow bushes. In fact, if it weren't for horse tracks it would be very difficult to follow the path at times. We begin a series of fords across some beautiful water and captivating glens. Fallen timber provides enough mass to block the stream and to create deep, achingly clear pools. I look for fish but I don't see any.

Up to this point Bailey has been able to ford the stream without too much difficulty. She's a filthy mess with sand clinging to her belly, but she's definitely not complaining. Deeper riffles have her hesitating before she selects a route that inevitably leads to dashes and jumps in hopes that she won't get wet—fond hopes.

After another ford I stop to look back at Bailey and then turn around, gauging the trail ahead. It's at that moment that I spy a moose track among hoof marks by the horses. Moose can be very cantankerous, as I've found out too many times.

Once I was hiking a well-used trail up Mount Timpanogos outside Robert Redford's Sundance Resort, in Utah, on a radiantly sunny September morning. Impenetrable shrubbery along the trail hid a delightfully splashing creek. Somehow as the trail swung close to the creek, a bull moose either heard me or picked up my scent. In a second it came crashing through branches, mud, and muck, hell-bent on flattening me. Fortunately a huge silvered aspen that had fallen years before blocked his way, allowing me time to escape. I'll never forget the sound of his agitated grunting and branches snapping left and right as the bull honed in on me.

Willows lining Pilgrim Creek Trail are perfect habitat for these ungainly giants. Not only do they obscure the sides of the trail, but they also block line of sight since the trail twists and dips. The effect is similar to walking through a narrow, two-foot-wide corridor with a ten-foot-high ceiling that drapes over the trail. It's almost like a tunnel.

At one blind corner I stop and unhook my pepper spray from the pack's harness. We know grizzly and moose have been this way—and recently, given the different tracks. We would have no way of knowing if a moose is bedded down alongside the trail, or whether a grizzly has a kill cached but a few feet from our path. Without saying a word to one another, conversation is suddenly louder. Our calls to Bailey become shouts when almost a whisper would do. My whistles

Moose often reach humongous proportions. This bull is in the process of cleaning the velvet from his antlers.

calling her are shrill, distinctive against the sounds of stream and occasional wind gusting through the trees high up. We feel this spontaneous urge to clap our hands, loudly.

Looking up the trail it's not getting any better. Our two-foot-wide trail just plows continuously through eight- to ten-foot-high willows, with few breaks. We feel channeled in a maze with no ability to anticipate whatever lurks on the other side of the screen. Anxiousness is rising, quelled only by pepper spray in hand, a palliative to our psyches. Goodness, if a bear or moose came crashing out of the willows, we'd thoroughly douse ourselves in spray before we ever knew what was happening. And Bailey would, no doubt, come screaming back for protection; a tidy little morsel luring a bear ever closer.

Finally, Pilgrim Creek Trail re-crosses its namesake and we rejoice in open river and the chance to take our bearings. Canyon walls squeeze

Pilgrim Creek, quickening its course and washing away sediment and soil that willows need to thrive. But, there's a price to pay for the creek's open, airy feeling. The trail now crosses and re-crosses Pilgrim Creek repeatedly, adding to Bailey's consternation. The waters have changed from a lazy, meandering creek down on the floodplain to a full-on mountain stream with power, intent on a specific direction and gathering force to reach this destination posthaste.

A little knoll on the creek sits warming in the ever-rising sun, inviting us to linger, but the price is yet another crossing. By now we've given up on trying to keep our boots from becoming sopping wet, so we ford Pilgrim Creek one more time on top of several fortunately placed rocks. Free of the willows we have a chance to take stock of our surroundings. We've progressively penetrated deeper into the Teton Wilderness and can anticipate reaching the point where Pilgrim Creek Trail divides into three separate paths all eventually destined to intersect Wildcat Peak Trail.

Basking in the embrace of the friendly sun, I cherish simply being in this magnificent wilderness. We've traveled far, expending a lot of time and money to reach the Tetons, but the cost has been worth it. In fact, it seems like a downright bargain in this lonesome canyon. We're experiencing the epitome of a wilderness outing. There are no mechanical intrusions or crowding by hordes of people intent on seeing spectacular sights. No, those types are miles over to the west of Pilgrim Mountain, fighting each other for their share of John D. Rockefeller Jr. Memorial Parkway.

At last we've reached pristine wildness virtually untrammeled by man. Except for the packer's camp we've seen no one, nor will we the remainder of this trip. But it isn't just the absence of people that enriches our wilderness experience. It's the entire chaotic ensemble of forest, creek, sun, trees, shrubs, sky, wind, and all other manifestations of life perfectly coalescing in our rest break there on that little knoll. The moment is a metaphor for wildness.

It isn't the threat of big mammals and ferocious carnivores that gives Pilgrim Creek a healthy dose of wildness, although their nearness adds a fine edge to what we're enjoying. It's more the realization that we made our way here by ourselves, under our own power. Few visitors, an almost infinitesimal number considering the millions who drive through the park each year, will ever venture to Pilgrim Creek Trailhead, much less step foot down the trail or ford Pilgrim Creek. This isolation from human impact may give Pilgrim Creek a greater wildness quotient than even the Thorofare up in Yellowstone National Park.

Grizzly bears and moose add to the wild cachet of Pilgrim Creek. You don't have to see them, confront them, to appreciate their presence. Their tracks are sufficient to add a whopping dollop of adrenaline to our tongues. Imprints in the mud, on the very path we're walking, confirm the wild quality of Pilgrim Creek drainage and add to its enticing allure. Their tracks accentuate the wildness of our experience and make this outing distinctive compared to other wilderness forays enjoyed in other forests.

I look down on Bailey plopped flat out on her filthy, furry belly in the sun, squinting up at me, seeking reassurance. What's she thinking about all of this—wild animal smells she's only encountered occasionally before, deeper water than she has been called on to cross, parents all bedecked with strange canisters possessing just a hint of their evil, foul-smelling contents? What do animals think about wilderness? Her eagerness to tackle the

Grizzlies are big and powerful, capable of taking down animals as large as elk, moose, and bison. It is important that they are not surprised by hikers or hunters at close range because feeling threatened may lead them to attack.

tough stuff probably says it all. I think she's enjoying this as much, if not more, than we are.

At moments like this, even a cardboard-flavored sports bar tastes good while the blazing sun burns through our windproof shirts. No cares. No intrusions. No agenda. Nothing to do. We have the luxury of time to enjoy life as it's meant to be lived.

Up and over the knoll we climb, seeking more adventure and desperately hoping that the willow curtain won't come crashing back. It's time for another ford and then the trail closes in again. Only this time there's something in the air that's indefinable; just a hint of danger that we can't really express. The willow corridor is no different than the one we've just traveled. Intuitively, something isn't right, but I can't quite put my finger on it. Bailey gives no overt indication that something's wrong. She just stands there dripping, with nose held slightly higher as she tests the air, not getting very far away from us.

It's been more than enough, this foray into wildness. Time to return while the memory is positive rather than calamitous. We head back over the knoll and splash across the narrowed stream while Bailey attempts to make her own soggy way. Unfortunately for her, Pilgrim Creek is running seriously swift and deep at this crossing. She hit rocks in the stream just right on the way over, but coming back presents a whole new puzzle.

Now's the time for this puppy to sink or swim.

Bailey runs frantically from one spot to the next, trying to figure out how to get across the creek. She's been lucky to this point, locating shallows and rocks that have kept her from swimming any length. We call encouragement, but she doesn't hear. Only fright masks her face. From one point to the next she runs, desperate to figure a way across. Finally she turns and runs back up trail, but my whistles bring her back.

Bailey tests a big rock right in front of a major current. I'm edging downstream in case she doesn't make it. Wet pads and claws gain no purchase and she slides onto several smaller rocks before momentum carries her into the main current. Snout just above water, she dog-paddles frantically—fighting swift water and a vacuum of footholds. She paddles strongly enough that there's little drift and then suddenly, her paws are grasping for anything they can cling on to. She's made it, albeit as one very wet dog, clambering up on the rocky shore.

"Shake! Shake!"

Bailey's learned this word from bathing and she gathers herself before flinging water all over the place. The victorious heroine puts herself in order, spraying us in the process. It's a pretty fancy strut that comes next as she heads down trail. It may seem like a small moment, but it was quite the escapade to Bailey, and one filled with adrenaline for all of us. After conquering this challenge there will be no going back. She's earned her trail dog certification. I begin to chuckle to myself as her skinny, wet bowlegs begin the march down trail.

But then I freeze.

There, in the mud, is another grizzly bear track like those we'd seen at the trailhead—only this one is headed downstream instead of up. Wildness comes slamming back and we again return to a state of hypervigilance, ready for whatever adventure may part the willows along Pilgrim Creek.

Several days later we stop to visit friends in Colorado Springs. At dinner they share a newspaper article about mountain bikers who, on the *same* day Bailey was hiking Pilgrim Creek with us, encountered a grizzly along a trail above Brooks Lake by Pinnacle Buttes. Roughly five miles from Togwotee Pass, and some thirty miles east of Grand Teton National Park and Pilgrim Creek, the Teton Wilderness serves up an alluring mosaic of mountain lakes and loop trails.

The September 6, 2004, Associated Press article, headlined MOUNTAIN BIKER SURVIVES HARROWING GRIZZLY ATTACK, read:

> *Kirk Speckhals escaped his encounter without a scratch; he had only four dirt marks from the bear's claws on his forearm, a punctured bicycle tire and a bent rim. Speckhals gave credit to [Tom] Foley [his companion], who carried his can of spray on his hip, for saving his life. "I was on the ground with the bear on top of me," Speckhals said. "I was waiting for a bone-crunching*

bite. I was ready to die." . . . Foley arrived to see the bear sitting atop his friend . . . With pepper spray drawn, he advanced to within 15 feet and fired.

According to the article, Speckhals normally never carried bear spray, so he had been methodically ringing his bicycle bell to announce his whereabouts to any bears in the area. Unfortunately this particular grizzly never heard it, and Speckhals endured an intimate encounter of the furry kind. He was lucky that Foley brought spray along, but the spray was almost not enough:

The bear got off his friend but turned and began circling Foley who was still spraying in the animal's face . . . With perhaps a second's worth of spray left, Foley tried a new tactic. He yelled at the bear at the top of his lungs. "I could tell his eyes changed," Foley said. "I knew it was over. All of a sudden he took off."

Grizzly bears in the lower forty-eight states do not have the luxury of salmon runs as do coastal bears, thus they are constantly looking for food, consisting mostly of roots, tubers, and greens. Not an easy life. No wonder they are known for having a bad attitude!

I swallow my greasy cheese quesadilla with an uncomfortable gulp and chase it down with another swig of my margarita. This trail is precisely the alternative trail we considered instead of Pilgrim Creek. It was only the extra road mileage we would have had to drive—forty-five miles one way—to reach Brooks Lake that ultimately shunted us to Pilgrim Creek. If we had foregone Pilgrim Creek it might have been us confronting the grizzly. On the other hand, perhaps something larger was at play? Something intuitive that tipped the scales toward a trail where a grizzly had already left its imprint before lumbering into an impenetrable screen of willows.

Bailey simply went out for a little adventurous backcountry excursion. Little did this princess-turned-tough-guy know that danger was waiting—or did she?

4 ℮

EARS BACK; CUB AT SIDE

A massive pile of minutes-old gooey-purple bear scat blocks the trail. Slightly steaming, it's very, *very* fresh and about the size of a small pumpkin, befitting this late-October day. Glancing wildly around to detect any lurking black bear, my early warning system relaxes a smidgen since the coast seems to be clear. No large dark lump is partially hidden at forest's edge, but there's a distinct hint of danger in the air. I slowly turn 360 degrees, carefully measuring the fine mess I've gotten into. Well-fed bears in the Shenandoah Mountains can easily reach 300 pounds, and judging by this pile of poop, whoever left it is outrageously gigantic.

My mouth becomes as parched as Death Valley while tension riddles my rigid body. I'm trying to stare through a particularly wicked tangle of brush forty-five feet to the south which could easily conceal a sofa-size bruin. Oak and hickory trees surrounding this grassy mountain meadow have already lost most of their crumpled rust-brown leaves, so it's nearly impossible to step without emitting a resoundingly loud *crrrrunch*. If a bear is stalking me, any movement should be all too apparent.

Whatever left such a monstrous load must be the undisputed king of Shenandoah National Park. *Ursus americanus* is out there somewhere, and, judging by a new world record for bear scat at the tip of my scuffed boot, it has been gorging big-time on various grasses, berries, and nuts. The perpetrator has to be a trophy specimen.

Nothing goes to waste in nature. Here a butterfly is foraging a scat pile for nutrients.

Snapping to attention as conscious thoughts merge with a misty cloud of intuition, pungent fragrances flood my nose—damp grasses on this chilly morning, the faint decomposition of freshly fallen oak leaves, rank stench of a hulking mammal recently passed, punky wood smoke from a distant campfire, soil oozing with dew, and terror rapidly seeping out of my pores. My pulse has shot up so high I'm almost panting. Steam dissipates in gossamer clouds from damp vegetation feeling that first magical touch of morning sun while I search the scraggly brush pile fifteen yards away for danger. A bear is obviously nearby, but where? Is it about to charge?

If I'm going to continue on this trail I will have to negotiate a black bear maze. The path leaves this open meadow for an alleyway of six-foot-high oaks. Each side of the trail is bracketed by huge pillows of oaks flowing off the hillsides. Their leaves may be gone, but these thickets are still impenetrable . . . except to bears. Better conditions for an ugly ambush are difficult to imagine.

It's just too quiet—unnaturally silent. But, I'm not about to tuck tail and run. There's really no choice but to plunge headlong down the trail fenced in by its straitjacket of glossy oak branches. Still, I'm wary about what predatory monster may be hidden just ahead.

Birds and squirrels that normally infest these Appalachian hills are suddenly nowhere to be heard, much less seen. Usually they are squawking up a storm. Where has everyone gone? What do they know that I don't—sitting up high in the relative safety of lofty branches, watching an innocent pilgrim about to collide with the unknown? A sense of extreme peril swarms over me. I'm out here all alone armed with nothing more than a wad of tissue, aspirin, matches, a year-old candy bar, and a sandwich. I'd give a king's ransom for a can of pepper spray.

Mr. Hotshot Outdoorsman didn't bring the bear spray with him today by deliberate choice. Prior encounters with bruins in this park came off pretty predictably—they all scooted off like flight-crazy bottle rockets just as soon as they saw me. With fall's chill I decided to dump the pepper spray in order to carry an extra shirt and a bit more water because this hike is on the long side. I didn't realize how lonesome a mountain meadow could be with the Skyline Parkway so near; how intimidating trophy-bear scat can be with no one around.

Fall is a perfect time for bagging peaks and little adrenaline-laced adventures in Appalachian bear country. Shenandoah National Park in Virginia's Blue Ridge Mountains comprises three hundred square miles of delightful mountain surprises—enchanted hollows

When a bear snaps its jaws it is saying "back off."

and dripping glens; rolling hills occasionally spiked with rocky peaks; graceful, murmuring streams wending their way to the Shenandoah River; and stunning views east and west toward verdant valleys. Routes tend to be upside-down because major trailheads are located on or near the Appalachian crest or the ever-popular Skyline Drive. Hiking paths drop precipitously toward valley floors flowing like water off this ancient mountain chain. The Appalachian Trail runs perpendicular to the side trails. It plods relentlessly northward toward Maine.

Inverted hiking takes some getting used to—it's akin to adventuring out west in canyon country. In early fall Shenandoah treks begin with cool, even cold, temperatures that rise rapidly while you stroll down to balmier climes. As a result, hikers wear most of their clothing at the start of each trek before progressively shedding insulation as they lose precious elevation but gain warmth. On reaching turnaround points near the base of the Appalachian Mountains, an unpleasant surprise awaits like a sharp slap across the face: That daypack has managed to grow to twice its size after you've removed all of those comfortable fleece layers, and suddenly, you're faced with the physical challenge of climbing *up* to a distant crest with a now massive weight on your back—quite the uncomfortable predicament.

Having started at Browns Gap—2,600 feet elevation—located on the southern end of Shenandoah National Park, I follow the Appalachian Trail north for about a half-mile before heading west on Rockytop Trail. The plan is to chase this route seven winding miles and roughly 1,200 feet in elevation loss down to Big Run Portal Trail before returning back up to the paved road bisecting this park. By wilderness adventure standards this isn't a major league hike in terms of mileage and elevation gain. Nonetheless, it's a significant challenge in Shenandoah National Park that trumps many trails in either evergreen forest or desert canyon lands during fall. If you hit it just right, the Blue Ridge Mountains are ablaze with a brilliant mosaic of crimson, yellow, and orange colors when foliage reaches its peak.

A little more than a mile from one of the busiest roads in the national park system—Skyline Drive—and only several miles from homes visible in the distance, for all intents and purposes I'm deep in wilderness on this mountainside perch. Nonetheless, the threat of a marauding bear is a reality, not a virtual experience. It's precisely this thrilling opportunity to walk in and with the wild that brings me here among gnarly tree skeletons hardening off for the winter. Gathering resolve, calmed by the embrace of earth and forest, and hypersensitive to any unusual sound, movement, or smell, this is exactly the sort of thrill that anyone deserves in Virginia's spectacular woods.

Wilderness adventuring often serves up generous portions of unanticipated encounters such as my chance run-in with steaming bear scat. I'm half sad, half happy. I would have liked to see this bear up close just to validate its inconceivable bulk. Imagine having the heart-pumping, armpit-drenching chance to stare it down from across Rockytop's placid meadow. On the other hand, given the vaporizing mound's dimensions, it's probably better that we didn't meet face-to-face. This bear is huge, probably three to four times bigger than me.

Unexpected surprises like this from backcountry rambles renew outdoor lovers' spirits, helping us to break out of daily doldrums and to live, breathe, think, smell, hear, and react as we did when we lived close to the earth. I feel charged with electricity and admittedly, a niggling little bit of fear—but not enough to prevent me from heading down trail. An unanticipated confrontation with smoldering bear scat has simply brought back a lot of very valuable abilities grown dormant from urban living. And, there's a very simple beauty to it all. I fit in this grassy clearing on the shoulder of Rockytop Mountain as much as the naked oak trees, darting gray birds, creeping burgundy-leafed vines, hollows laced with green junipers, and hazy fall skies.

Once again I'm sensitive to a serious threat from a large mammal in hyperphagia—an omnivore greedily consuming every calorie possible, every morsel no matter how big or small; plants, rodents, or human beings—in order to survive winter's hibernation. I cannot afford to rely on only one or two human defense mechanisms. All are vitally needed, and needed now. I have to look out for me. The Park Service cannot do it. A call on a cell phone would be too late. It's down to wits, wisdom, and experience.

After adrenaline subsides, it goes that much better because of a lucky encounter. Shucking off cares and concerns from the city, I focus on the

An alert black bear in a young lodgepole pine forest.

here and now, on the forest and all that nature offers. Formerly big issues clouding my brain shrink back into proportion to what they really are—minutiae that can be addressed back in the city. They will wait while I splash across crystal-clear Big Run Creek just before it enters the South Fork of the Shenandoah River. Anxieties and worries of this world can go on hold while I marvel at brilliant yellow leaves spread like a quilt on Big Run Creek. Dilemmas of my life will have to leave a voice mail, because I am too busy relishing a ridgeline saunter through warming sun past hidden famished omnivores, toward a distant shimmering stream dropping off the Appalachian Mountains.

My alarm at surprising *Ursus americanus*, or black bear, on Rockytop Trail just before it dens for the winter kindles an interesting thought. Bears are forever focused on filling their distended bellies with any tasty, even raunchy, morsel they can find. After hibernating for a good four to six months, they emerge ravenous and desperate to find sustenance. In spring this makes them fairly indiscriminating regarding when, what, or where they eat. A bloated, smelly elk carcass is cause to rejoice; a convenient garbage can stuffed to the brim with rotting leftovers is too good to pass up. As winter nears, their instincts tell them to gorge because it's going to be an eternity until that next meal rolls around. And in between summer and autumn the land showers a bounty of food to build fat reserves, spelling the difference between making another spring or not.

Knowing that bears are very adept at focusing on one thing in fall—food—partially explains my apprehension on Rockytop Trail. I'm really not interested in becoming a convenient way for some black bear to tide himself over during the winter, as much as I love bruins. Hyperphagia is nothing to fool around with, especially when a bear doesn't feel sufficiently fed to survive winter. Instinct-driven hyperphagia raises the odds that a bear will go after a biped, something that it normally would have avoided at all costs. A frantic and instinctive need for food could overrule a bear's innate need for safety. That's the virtual image flitting through my mind as I scan this serene meadow, ever alert for an incoming mass of muscle, viselike jaws, and powerful canines.

In contrast to the fall, spring and summer have two major distractions—cubs and reproduction—that compete with food as the number-one bear priority. Females are busy shepherding newborn or yearling cubs toward safe food sources. They're concentrating on lessons their mothers taught them about food, conveying these to their offspring, and showing their cubs fresh twists on knowledge passed down through the generations. Meanwhile, males and females without cubs fight a battle between two overpowering drives—to eat and to procreate. After they relieve winter's enormous calorie deficit, their minds turn to mush as breeding season nears.

Spring, summer, or fall—there probably isn't any good season to surprise a bear when you're alone, whether with firepower or without. Bears are always hungry, almost embarrassingly so. An unexpected human encounter may inadvertently rearrange their synapses. Suddenly you're seen as a convenient way to overcome a compelling and insatiable craving gnawing at their stomachs. And why shouldn't they capitalize on unexpected manna from bear heaven? There's no question they're bigger than you. Furthermore, bears can smell that fear riddling your body—all of those pheromones flooding out your pores. Yes, a person alone in the field is always tempting fate regardless of the season.

Speed forward seven months to April when Shenandoah National Park is enjoying a crescendo of new spring growth. Life is virtually smothering the Appalachian Mountains. Humidity is rising as fertile valley fields and deciduous forest draped on mountain ridges soak up sunny warmth. The cauldron is just beginning to boil. It will reach a crescendo of frequent, even daily, thunderstorms, returning each molecule of water in a never-ending cycle. It's time to get out for a hike while I can avoid stewing in my own juices and enjoy the phenomenal botanical diversity of ancient East Coast mountains.

Riprap Trail is located just north of mile marker 90 along Skyline Drive. It's one of those little, nondescript pullouts that not many people see in their big hurry to speed between Blackrock Gap and Beagle Gap. But I've noticed it—the perfect hiding spot to sequester my car on the southern end of Shenandoah National Park. Any wayward traveler intent on watching something other than the road will inadvertently take out the protective cushion of three cars parked north of me. That three other vehicles are already parked is not a good omen. I've gotten an unusually late start and it's already in the midseventies with humidity drenching at 85 percent.

Mountain crest, Appalachian Trail, and Skyline Drive intimately intertwine above the Shenandoah Valley. The Appalachian Trail climbs for a bit less than a half-mile paralleling Skyline Drive to the west. It's not entirely unpleasant walking this close alongside a busy parkway. Shenandoah National Park's speed limit, aggressive law enforcement, and natural twists and turns keep traffic intrusion to a minimum, except when *Dukes of Hazzard*-like muscle cars roar past. They risk attracting the attention of a different kind of Smokey the Bear. Despite being so close to the road, I'm attuned to the wonderful background music of gently singing birds, wind softly sighing through the trees, and veritable ambrosia of earthly scents. In less than ten minutes, Riprap Trail enters from the west. From here on I'm on autopilot—no schedule or interruptions, just flowing with the mountain into Riprap Hollow. Down, that is, after a gentle little climb to Calvary Rocks—a stunning jumble of quartz outcroppings—and Chimney Rock. Mesmerized by silence, the forest's green embrace, and the joy of stretching my legs, the brilliant white quartz only seems like pretty eye candy. Its geologic significance soars right over my head.

That's when death comes calling. Or slithering.

Sliding by Chimney Rock with almost no thoughts or cares on my radar screen, I just happen to glance down behind my right leg as it brushes inches away from the quartz outcrop. Why I turn and look down isn't clear, but what I see is frighteningly unmistakable. A fat, five-foot-long timber rattlesnake all mottled black-gray and green lays coiled just behind a beach ball–size chunk of rock along the trail. Instinctively I fade, almost stumble to the left and spin to confront the serpent. The snake just sits there with its tongue flicking out. Luckily there's no death rattle, no aggressive S-shaped coiling as a prelude to striking. Like a cat taking a sunny nap on a cold winter's day, the snake just maintains a comfortable repose.

I can't quite figure out why I glanced down and slightly behind me. Perhaps it was a slight movement that registered subconsciously. Maybe not-so-dormant instincts were scanning for something—a scent, sound, vibration, spiritual presence, or sudden change in behavior by birds, chipmunks, and insects? Who

Most often a rattlesnake will give plenty of warning before it strikes.

knows? Does it really matter? The snake respects my space. It shows no aggression and asks for none. We stare at each other eye to eye from six feet away. Our telepathy is unambiguous—you leave me alone and I'll leave you alone.

Bound for a dark shady tunnel formed by Cold Spring Hollow, I make tracks toward its cooling shade and precious water. Only thirty yards after leaving the quartz pile, pandemonium breaks loose as irate jays, startled flickers, and obstreperous nutcrackers squawk about the serpent. They have reason to chatter on this avian singing wire—either eggs or young wait nearby in nests. What a phenomenal difference a predator makes in the wilderness atmosphere. Surrounding life rises with primal instinct to defend the realm while I gradually switch back to autopilot.

Gliding down the trail I begin to notice several ottoman-size holes in the earth. Someone or something seems to have been digging throughout forest duff lining the trail. The excavations are impressively deep in places. I'm trying to understand what the architect was looking for. Mushrooms? Nope—too dry. Pinecones? Nope—pines are too few and far between. Lily, onion, or other edible bulbs? Perhaps, but there's no discarded green leafy vegetation strewn about to confirm this supposition. Chipmunks? No—these excavations are too distant from protective rocks and fallen logs. Besides, there's too much dirt moved for it to be small mammals or rodents. Feral pigs going after truffles? Ahead I can see another series of mystery diggings strewn on either side of the trail. What's going on here?

Cold Spring Hollow is about to drop precipitously into Riprap Hollow, when all of a sudden my wrist is on fire as well as one hypersensitive butt cheek. *Ouch!* Searing pain in both spots has my complete attention. It feels like someone is taking a red-hot poker and burning it into my flesh. In another nanosecond I'm hopping around trying to swat wasps off my wrist and fanny before breaking into a full-out run down trail. After running flat-out for twenty-five yards, my desperate, panicked dash seems to have left the horde of wasps behind, so I stop to survey the damage. An egg-size welt is rising on my wrist; I can only imagine what my butt must look like just under my shorts. It still feels like someone is pushing and twisting an ice pick in each location.

Fortunately I'm carrying a number of Benadryl tablets for just such an emergency. I shred the medication's plastic wrapper while groping frantically for my bottle of water. Meanwhile, the lump on my wrist continues to rise as an ugly, purple-red, silver dollar–size mound inflates. I pop a pill knowing that the next twenty minutes are not going to be much fun until the medication kicks in. Suddenly sweat is dripping off my forehead, my palms are drenched, and I'm feeling very light-headed. Shock is just what I don't need out here in the wilderness, so I sit down to rest until the medicine flushes through my veins. Eventually equilibrium returns and I'm able to carry on as planned.

TRAVELING SAFELY IN THE WOODS

No matter how carefully people walk in the wilderness, there is always a chance that something is going to go wrong even though they were exercising prudent caution. Consequently, there is a great deal of wisdom in routinely carrying essentials to deal with unanticipated surprises that crop up. Mountain lore suggests carrying ten essentials, although the exact number and list of essentials varies from expert to expert. The Mountaineers, a well-known outdoor recreation organization in the Pacific Northwest, suggests carrying the following items on every venture into the backcountry. This list and other precautions are available at their Web site, www.mountaineers.org/main/essentials.html:

1. Navigation (map and compass)
2. Sun protection
3. Insulation (extra clothing)
4. Illumination (flashlight/headlamp)
5. First-aid supplies
6. Fire
7. Repair kit and tools
8. Nutrition (extra food)

9. Hydration (extra water)

10. Emergency shelter

None of the preceding substitutes for common sense. In fact, it takes common sense to determine which items to add to these ten essentials and which to delete depending on the trail conditions that may be encountered.

Personally, I think the three most promising essentials in cool weather are a wool/synthetic hat, gloves, and a wind/rain shell. It's impossible to know when a storm will suddenly materialize. Since you lose roughly 50 percent of your heat through your head, it pays to carry an insulating cap. Gloves increase heat retention to the extremities while a shell fends off wind and rain that can rob a person of life-giving warmth. In hot weather, sun protection and an abundant water supply are foremost on my mind.

Regardless of the weather I always carry a little kit of basic first-aid supplies (e.g., Motrin, Benadryl, and bandages), tissues and toilet paper, a knife, matches, and several candy bars (seems like I'm always adding new candy bars). In winter I add extra fire starters (i.e., butane lighter and pitch-laden sticks), as well as extra clothing sufficient to allow me to survive a night outdoors. Due to these precautions my pack sometimes weighs more or is decidedly bulky compared to others who laugh in the face of fate, but I've always made it back alive.

It's the erroneous assumptions that get people into trouble, so pack more than appears needed under the conditions. The following example illustrates why:

I was deep in Olympic National Park along the Quinault River Trail on a perfectly sunny day. Washington

State had been enjoying record warm weather. No storms were forecast for several more days. Nonetheless, a massive thunderstorm sprung up unexpectedly, unleashing a deluge which rapidly lowered the ambient temperature.

One hour after this storm began I ran into a young woman and man struggling to hike five more miles to the trailhead. Because the weather had been so perfect, he'd decided to forego his rain gear. Bad decision. He was soaked and miserably cold, on the verge of hypothermia. He did have a wool cap that was keeping him going. His companion had thoughtfully brought her rain suit and was watching over him with great angst as they tried to speed back to safety. How much does a lightweight raincoat weigh? Did it make sense to jeopardize one's life to save a half-pound?

Always take more than you think you will need.

There's perhaps another mile to drop down Riprap Hollow's drainage and confluence with Meadow Run, so I have plenty of time to nurse my wounds and conjecture about what happened back there. The facts begin to come together—and they point to one particular forest culprit: a bear. Some four-legged shaggy beast has methodically traversed along Riprap Trail digging up wasp nests while seeking succulent goodies from the underground hives. A few wasp survivors remain on guard and ready to protect the remnants of their nests from any large biped or quadruped ambling down the trail. Only this time the wasps are on the offensive.

Black bears may not be actually visible here in the daylight, but their handiwork is all too readable now that I've been stung a couple times. It was easy for them to tackle wasps or bees with their shaggy coats. In contrast, I'm almost defenseless. The wasp bites continue to throb as I find a place to sit down and relax for lunch. I feel like I've run the gauntlet— first a monster rattlesnake and now a surprise attack from infuriated wasps.

Hard to believe this black bear cub just six months earlier weighed only ten to sixteen ounces at birth and was just eight inches in length.

Plus, I have to run the course a second time in order to return to my car. A thought progressively grows that takes the polish off what is normally a serene Riprap Hollow.

Will I be able to get back safely?

Turning to go, I begin to prepare mentally for what lies ahead. Now I'm climbing steeply uphill and I'll have to really run to get through land mines of furious wasps. Twenty minutes after starting back up I reach the first battlefield and try to race to safety several yards away. Almost as soon as I'm fifteen feet from the nests, wasps begin descending and I'm able to swat them away while making a run for it. This is repeated twice more until Cold Spring Hollow is left for the ridge formed by Calvary Rocks and Chimney Rock. Each time I approach a devastated underground nest, wasp bombers come diving toward me. Only one little bastard gets through my defenses.

Chimney Rock has its own challenge and I slow to a crawl in anticipation of the rattlesnake. Hopefully by now, the timber rattler has slithered off to other destinations. Nonetheless I'm walking very cautiously to avoid the same surprise I had on the way in. Then around a bend in the trail just north of Calvary Rocks I spy the rattler one foot off the main path. It's stretched out to some five-plus feet, slowly sliding through the underbrush. If I hadn't been looking for it I would never have seen it— absolutely perfect camouflage.

Somehow this last wild encounter fits in perfectly with a totally hair-raising day. I slump into my car seat and crank the air-conditioning on full blast. While waiting for it to chill the stuffy humidity crammed into an oppressive minigreenhouse, there's a moment to reflect. On this most ancient of mountain ranges I thought about others who have trod this mountain hundreds of years before with the same intense alertness, expecting something to abruptly jump out at them. In the final analysis the unknown had left a sweet taste of adventure lingering on my palate. What a grand hike it turned out to be.

Two weeks after being mugged by wasps I have another chance to seek adventure at Shenandoah National Park. My pack loaded with water, snacks, and a bite for lunch, I push off on the Appalachian Trail running parallel to Skyline Drive. Immediately the path begins climbing Bear Den Mountain. Not a car goes by on the parkway while I hike due north. How few times does this familiar formula repeat itself in the course of a

Black bears inhabit forest and swamps of North America ranging in elevation from sea level to 10,000 feet. They can be so secretive that they are often found in city parks and neighborhoods without anyone knowing they are there.

year? Inevitably I run into dismal gray days, unexpected thunderstorms, snow squalls, hurricane winds, and other weather challenges; however, memories of glorious moments such as this capture what I remember most about backcountry adventuring.

In thirty minutes I can see Calf Mountain Shelter—a beacon of warmth and safety to thru-hikers on the Appalachian Trail. Supposedly there's a spring nearby, but I'm not stopping for water because I have all I need on my back. This shelter is primarily for cooking and emergency conditions. Tent sites surround the shelter maintained by the Potomac Appalachian Trail Club. If the shelter could talk, I can only imagine the funny stories it would tell . . .

Crash! Bam! Boom!

I spin around to see a solid black sow and cub come racing downhill, running across the trail directly in front of me and crashing noisily through the undergrowth. Where they came from I'll never know. Talk about getting up close and personal! The smell of foul stomach acid on the sow's lips combined with the stench of their filthy, matted fur is almost too much to handle. The mother's claws—not grizzly razor blades, but stout monsters—are extended and ready for action. The cub's tongue whips and flops from side to side in their frantic dash to beat me on the trail. The encounter is so unexpected that I consider pinching myself. They could not have crossed more than ten feet in front of me.

LUCK OF THE DRAW

Bill Schuette, author of *White Blaze Fever*, hiked the length of the Appalachian Trail—all 2,167 miles from Springer Mountain, Georgia, to Katahdin, Maine. In his book, Schuette recounts how eager he was to see a bear. After 846 miles on the trail he reached Calf Mountain Shelter. Despite having covered almost 40 percent of the Appalachian Trail, he had inexplicably registered no sightings—this is after having traipsed through bear-infested Great Smoky Mountains National Park.

That night, a young hiker came in and reported a bear sighting—appropriately enough, since Bear Den Mountain is only a stone's throw down the trail. Some eighty miles later and just short of Elkwallow Gap, Schuette had his first black bear encounter, which he described as ". . . an awesome sight."

Even in areas renowned for bears, luck plays an important role in whether people enjoy a sighting. It's possible to follow all of the steps necessary to raise the probability of seeing a bear—choosing the right location where bears have been sighted before; going at dawn or dusk; and walking as noiselessly as possible—and still miss out.

However, there is one factor that significantly increases the likelihood of a bear sighting: The more you get outdoors in bear country, the greater the odds that eventually, you will see a bear.

What phenomenal luck! But it's probably more than coincidence. The shelter undoubtedly attracts bears because of the campers who cook meals in or around the structure. Carelessness with food ultimately habituates bears to an unexpected larder. Soon it becomes easier to mug campers than to forage. This sow had probably been positively reinforced in the past and now she was teaching her cub about how to negotiate interactions with humans in order to safely bully food from them. It's a lot easier to walk to a place known to provide delectable treats than to spend all day in the hot sun searching for a vegetarian meal.

Lush trailside growth—some areas up to seven feet tall—lines the trail, which drops and bends around a corner. The bears ran into this copse of brush and I can't see them, but I can hear them causing a ruckus. Then silence reigns over this little hollow. Should I go forward, or retreat?—It's tough to tell. Intellectually I know that hikers should do everything in their power to avoid encountering a sow with her cub. In this case, I'm thinking that the drama was over before it began. The sow

On the East Coast the vast majority of black bears are black colored, thus the name. As one moves to the western U.S. the color lightens and approximately half the bears are a brown color.

should have charged me when we first intersected, and by all rights, this very minute I should be curled up in a ball, trying to play dead as she mauls me. Or, I should already be a bloody mess lying on my back, helplessly staring up at a gently undulating parrot-green canopy of leaves overhead.

On the other hand, the sow may be waiting to see if I press the point. She may be thinking about the treats that lie in the pack on my back. But, if I continue to present a threat to her cub, she may just come over and neutralize me to show her cub how you handle pesky humans. I stand silently, mulling over the matter.

How lucky do I feel today?

Desire to keep going overrules safety, so I walk another fifty feet down the trail. I hear more stirring in bushes twenty yards away, so I stop. Then silence closes in again. Birds have stopped calling. Squirrels are hunkered down. Even the breeze goes on hold. A little shiver crawls up my spine, but after a few minutes all signs of the bears evaporate. I walk another fifty feet to a little bend in the trail only to hear pounding and rustling in the bushes. It's as though someone is driving a Mack truck toward me. I brace for annihilation and then quiet blankets the glen.

Stupidly, I've worked myself into a position where either going forward or retreating carries possible bear reprisal. I'm not exactly certain of where they are, but from the recent rumble it's clear the sow isn't very pleased. I pick up several rocks from the path as a stupid defensive gesture, walk another thirty feet, and stop. Listen. Padded feet shuffle in one spot, and then through a break in the dark green leaves shadowed by overhanging limbs, I see the cub and sow.

At first I catch a glimpse of her furry butt, but then she swings around to face me head-on. Her cub, which is initially broadside, shifts accordingly, sticking to its mother like a moth on flypaper. It has this bewildered and terrified look in its eyes. It's either frantic with fear or with trepidation about what Mother is about to do. I can't see the sow's eyes because of a huge mass of broad leaves hanging down from a shrub, but I can see a bit of drool slip off her muzzle.

The best decision is for me to slowly back off and get out of there. However, I really want to keep hiking. So, placing one rock in my right hand I fire a missile that scatters in the brush and then another that thumps something—bear, tree limb, or rock—and falls silent.

It occurs to me that if I hit the cub with a rock, it is going to bawl, and that's going to set off the sow. Bad idea. My last fusillade must have hit the sow, but she didn't react. Okay . . . now what? I move along the trail another twenty feet and see that the path is headed

Climbing trees comes naturally to black bear cubs. This is how they escape enemies while mother defends them at the tree trunk.

right for where the sow and cub are hiding behind a porous screen of bushes. That doesn't look good. She's not going to give ground very easily, particularly since she knows she's got me outgunned. All of a sudden the isolation of a midweek hike isn't providing the return I was looking for.

Sometimes the better part of valor is backing off gracefully. I've pushed this just about as far as you can push a bear without enjoying a good measure of retaliation. I can't count on anyone coming along so that we can join forces. In the end I decide to begin backing up the trail very carefully to let the sow know I'm keeping my eyes on her. Tucking tail and retreating isn't my preferred choice, but the Charlottesville hospital is not somewhere that I want to be visiting today. Seconds later, back at the shelter's clearing, my anxiety drops a notch, but I'm still wary. Every five minutes or so as I descend Calf Mountain, I take a long glance behind to see what's coming. High drama is over for today and the bears aren't determined to escort me off Calf Mountain.

An enormous pile of scat, a stealthlike rattlesnake, carnage on wasp nests, and nearly getting bowled over by a freight train consisting of a distraught sow and her cub—these are treasures awaiting those who venture out into Appalachian bear country. They are precisely the sort of unknown factors that make backcountry rambles so alluring. Simply walking down a path without paying attention to what's going on around you can lead to some pretty serious repercussions. You rapidly begin to realize that rusty or dormant abilities—highly acute hearing, smell, sight, and physical reactions—are extremely valuable if you want to travel safely through the woods.

There is also a *chance* to see wildlife in action and to appreciate that for once, something other than humans dominates the food chain. It is very worthwhile for our society to be reminded that ours is not the only species on this planet that can hold sway. Humility generated by potential bear encounters helps to remind us that we share this planet with others.

Run-ins with *Ursus americanus* are definitely something to value and not to fear. But, make no mistake that everyone venturing down a wilderness

There is time for fun in a bear's life. Here a mother and cub are enjoying a spring day by wrestling.

trail has the responsibility to remain alert to unanticipated intersections with bears. If we're armed with foresight and caution, such encounters help to inspire our lives. They make us better people for the experience. That's a lot to be thankful for, and we owe a deep debt of gratitude to the furry creatures that live in our dreams—good and bad—and remain discreetly hidden as we plod along wilderness trails.

5

OSO CANELLA

Kabam . . .

A deafening crack splits the air, followed by a resounding boom echoing across a vast, gray-shrouded floodplain surrounding the little town of Talkeetna, Alaska. This isn't hunting season so it wasn't a rifle shot. Moments later a fusillade of heavy rain begins to fall, and shortly after that the sky opens up to a dismal deluge. Water literally runs everywhere, and Susitna River's formerly bone-dry oxbow channel outside our cabin collects parking lot–size, rain-dimpled ponds melding with each other as this section of the river springs to life once again. Rain savagely pelting the roof creates such a din that any conversation, even shouting, is hopeless. There really is no need for words, however, because the twelve of us on this rafting trip are all thinking the same thing: What a depressingly inauspicious way to begin a five-day trip rafting the Talkeetna River.

Two weeks ago, central Alaska experienced dramatic flooding of epic proportions from unusually intense summer rain. At home we watched National Oceanic and Atmospheric Administration (NOAA) reports about the growing calamity. It can take over a week for floodwaters to work their way down from high alpine and tundra country to forested lowlands. Rivers progressively dropped a good six feet or more once the flood was past. Would they fall enough to allow safe passage? This is our concern

Storms are a frequent occurrence along the beautiful and rugged Alaska Range.

since the Talkeetna squeezes into very narrow Devil's Canyon, a labyrinth of tortured walls and rockfall creating world-class white water.

A dozen souls huddle pathetically inside the hotel's lobby exchanging nervous glances, laughter, and false bravado while sharing bits and pieces about their lives. Our common bond is adventuring in the great Alaskan wilderness. What seemed like a wonderful idea six months earlier in the bucolic months of springtime now shows ragged edges. There were plenty of graphic warnings in the glossy Technicolor trip literature about stinging rain and blustery weather even in the depths of summer, but somehow we never envisioned massive sheets of water drowning everything. Are these intrepid adventurers, and their equipment, up to the task?

Great mounds of expensive paraphernalia spanning all the hues of a rainbow wait patiently to be packed in twenty-gallon-size dry bags. A guide will arrive shortly to distribute watertight containers and to review logistics. Too late to drop out now? A heavy-duty four-by-four midnight blue pickup skids to a gravel-scattering halt. Weighty footsteps clump up the wooden stairs, muffled by the pulsating racket of waterfalls cascading off the roof. Julie Boselli, our intrepid guide, muscles inside, accompanied by the dank scent of waterlogged earth and humid, refreshed air.

As the hotel's door slams shut, taunting *kaa-kaa-kaa* cries from a skein of ravens follow her. An eighty-mile trip down the wild and scenic Talkeetna River is about to begin.

Too-loó-uk. Raven. Indigenous Alaskans use a fittingly melodious name for a most intelligent bird. Considering the raven's many abilities and alluring persona, Too-loó-uk River Guides, based in Denali National Park, Alaska, has chosen a most appropriate moniker to symbolize this company's character.

Respected for their vast repertoire of calls, cunning, loyal monogamy, and phenomenal aerial capability, ravens often distinguish themselves as tricksters getting into mischief when searching for food and brightly colored objects to take back to their nests. They even quickly learn how to open zippers and to conquer sticky Velcro closures. Flying away with invaluable treasures and croaking loudly about their little Pyrrhic victories, it's difficult not to take great delight in their clever antics. But

Ravens are prevalent throughout Alaska. A pair will defend their territory against other ravens.

who is more richly rewarded—ravens for their plunder, or humans for the enjoyment?

Alaska proudly claims its fair share of ravens, a common sight along rivers, valleys, and floodplains. Competition is tough since eagles are equally prevalent in locales that ravens love. Nonetheless, their superior flying abilities help them avoid becoming easy pickings for eagles. Besides, there are too many other tasty morsels awaiting eagles. With brazenly bold spirits, ravens demonstrate immense courage, occasionally ganging up to chase off eagle interlopers. Wit and finesse trump size and strength in fierce battles.

Vibrant with life, the Talkeetna exemplifies pristinely vital wilderness and imagery of untrammeled nature. Charismatic fauna such as caribou, moose, wolves, porcupine, and beaver abound. A caribou escaping pesky flies and swarming mosquitoes is just as likely to come marching around the river's bend as a grizzly bear materializing from a yellow-green willow thicket above a flood-damp sandbar. Floating quietly down the Talkeetna increases the frequency of sightings, but even when animals disappear for a moment or two, the phenomenal beauty and scale of Alaskan wilderness rivets your attention.

Departure begins on the tarmac at Doug Geeting Aviation, a flying service offering logistics support for expeditions and general-service aviation assistance. Doug is perpetually decked out in droop-snoop sunglasses masking his eyes—the portal to his soul. He's wearing soiled, baggy chinos and a ragtag flannel shirt covering an ample belly that suggests one too many moose steaks. Doug is a curmudgeonly, aloof bush pilot who already made several trips the day before, dropping off guides and rafts. How he navigated given the horrendous weather is something to marvel at, but today, golden-yellow sun is shining brightly on Talkeetna's chilled river flats.

Under cloudless skies, Mount Denali shines like a radiant beacon robed in a fresh coat of pure white snow. Good day for flying. Several of us are more than a bit anxious about the flight into our launch point. Doug squeezes four people per trip in the single-engine, fifty-year-old plane that's held together by duct tape and baling wire. With great commotion he taxies down the runway only to have the passenger door unceremoniously flop open. We wrestle it shut and then we're off—haltingly, almost comically so, slowly up ten feet, twenty feet, and climbing with the engine roaring like a lawn mower. Doug constantly fiddles with the controls, trimming the ancient craft's engines and flight heading toward 6,100 feet elevation.

Anxious thoughts evaporate with the incredible grandeur spreading below our wings. A few houses, barns, and outhouses appear along forested riverbanks and small lakes, but within ten minutes only black-green wilderness forest carpets the earth, split by broad, sandy-gray canyons with plaited glacial rivers. Gradually lowland forests give way to rocky ridges covered in velvet-green, and mountain peaks, many of which are cloaked in a fragile coating of new snow—visitor-busters, according to our guides. The first sign of fresh snow signals the approach of fall, and snowbirds get out of town fast. High lakes no more than one or two acres in size abound, floating in a sea of green bushes—blueberry, cranberry, willow, and alder—below ridgetops.

Skimming fifty feet above a grassy ridge we drop precipitously like a falling stone into an enormous valley with wandering glacial streams flowing below. Banking hard left for the landing, Doug checks to make certain our cobblestone runway is clear, and then abruptly we are thirty, twenty, ten feet above the rutted, cobblestone-strewn ground and finally skid on a gravel-bar runway lined with dense willows only a foot from our wingtips. In a roaring crescendo, Doug wildly spins the plane 180 degrees, kicking up sand and gravel.

We're home.

Everyone pitches in to quickly unload the plane so that Doug can make his final flights, and then he's off roaring slowly up the runway, grabbing air and struggling over mountain ridges. Suddenly it is achingly quiet with only the sound of the swiftly moving river grinding gravel and sand thirty yards distant. One minute we were in the metropolis of Talkeetna and the next, almost one hundred miles away in the middle of nowhere. Chill air hangs heavily from last night's deep frost and the horrendous storm, but low temperatures are gradually moderating with abundant sun. It's going to be a fine day.

We grapple with wilderness shock—suddenly transported to deep wilderness without sufficient time for adjusting perceptually. The sun's orientation—relatively low on the horizon, yet shining brightly twenty-some hours—takes getting used to, and there is this vacuous sense of enormous country. We are five miles away from the glacier that produces the Talkeetna River, but distance is tough to comprehend. How high are the mountains welling up from the river bottom? How distant are the looming, snow-covered peaks? Time will soon calibrate our senses, so we meander around the launch site. The beach is rife with grizzly bear tracks and partially eaten salmon rotting in the sun—portents of wildlife viewing in the days to come.

Doug makes his last flight and final departure. Guess what? We're on our own. With everyone present and accounted for, our five guides begin safety instructions: The water is frigid, ripe with death; if you fall in, do not float and wait for rescue. Take care of yourself. You have roughly two minutes before you become numb with cold. After that, rescue becomes questionable, and you are headed toward becoming an unfortunate statistic. Swim for the nearest raft, swim for a boulder, swim for the shore gliding by; but don't wait for someone to save your sorry ass.

We randomly pick a raft—one guide on the oars and two to three people per guide—and then shove off, drifting slowly down the Talkeetna. Guides expertly negotiate the sandbar-laden braided channels that conspire to beach the rafts, although they aren't always successful. Then, we're rocking and bouncing, trying to free our crafts. Temperatures in the high sixties feel crisp as the rafts gain speed, helpful in leaving behind the few mosquitoes and flies we've encountered so far. Water laps rhythmically at our rafts while we gently weave the four miles down the Talkeetna.

Cobblestones and river rock, willow, alder, and blueberry bushes fight for space above a sandy beach as we glide to a halt. First camp is situated at the junction of a pristine nameless creek, perhaps twenty-five feet wide, and the Talkeetna. The creek flows strong and clear, laden with four-foot salmon spawning and carrying out their cycle of life. Tents are erected in a temporarily dry side channel surrounded by blueberry bushes weighed down with bulbous seasoned fruit and diminutive cranberry bushes just beginning to ripen. Bear scat, laced with pink salmon and blueberries, carpets game trails in and around camp. It's quintessential Alaskan wilderness.

With our sixteen-foot blue rafts bobbing gently in a quiet eddy off Talkeetna's main channel, the kitchen commandeers a seventy-foot crescent of gray sandy beach.

Summer is the time of plenty for caribou; unfortunately it is also the time for numerous pesky, biting insects.

As we all enjoy delicious hors d'oeuvres, Julie urges me to scan the hillside across the river if I want to see wildlife. According to Julie, that's where bears could be, so I keep binoculars in hand whenever I'm down on the beach.

A stout caribou with a trophy-size rack wanders silently upstream; dodging this cataract for a gentler riffle, keeping his antler-laden head turned into the slight breeze to defeat a few buzzing flies and mosquitoes, effortlessly fording the swift river, and detouring westward out of harm's way. Moments later, it appears that our bush plane is returning when a huge dark shadow races over the kitchen. A bald eagle swerves upward to the top branch of a fir and settles gracefully to watch for errant salmon. Scenes such as these continue to play out in moments of camaraderie over dinner and dessert in the middle of extraordinary wilderness.

❖

Next morning dawns clear and cold—27 degrees, to be exact—with frost everywhere. This feels more like Alaska, but soon the sun is penetrating our camp, warming the frigid air and enabling us to step back a bit from our blazing campfire on the outfitter's steel fire pan. With bacon sizzling, eggs on the griddle, and muffins in the Dutch oven, breakfast is promising—but I'm still focusing on the hillside. No sightings yet except for one lone caribou.

Most of the group is slow to get up this morning, a layover day for hiking and general exploration or for fishing. By mid-morning, chores are complete, lunches packed, camp tidied up, and we assemble for a hike toward an unnamed peak.

Grizzled Jim Hendrick will lead the way—and he should. He's the senior guide; the one with the most experience; the one owning the biggest gun. With adrenaline rising we follow a meandering game trail up a steep, undulating ridge from camp through all manner of blueberry and cranberry bushes, and taller shrubs like willow. Except for a hoof- and paw-beaten path on spongy emerald moss, the way is visually obscured; bushes slap us in the face as we try to penetrate tunnels created by bears and wolves.

The day turns hot and we continue to fight through and around a maze of bushes, clawing our way along a ridge and looking down upon the bountifully flowing clear creek along which our camp nestles. When salmon are running big-time we speculate about what this bear valley must look like, with cascading water frothing and flowing around and over protruding moss-covered boulders, fish fighting the currents, and furry paws conspiring to keep them from their destiny.

Eventually a high spot on the ridge affords a tremendous view of unnamed waterfalls dropping languorously twenty and thirty-plus feet into deep sapphire pools that gather and spend themselves with further falls. The only sounds are occasional wispy breezes through tundralike vegetation and a modulating distant roar of falls and river. Wildness permeates the mountainside.

The remainder of the afternoon I spend glassing the heavily vegetated hillside opposite camp. Nothing turns up. Dinner comes and goes. Nothing. Late that evening, dusk edging to twilight in the almost endless sunshine of Alaskan summer, I'm ready to head off to bed. Thirty feet away, ten people in our group are still hanging out around the kitchen's campfire on this crescent of beach. Should I take one last reconnaissance? Doesn't seem worth the trouble, but then I remember I may never be this way again. So, I take that proverbial final look.

Bingo!

A colossal grizzly is sauntering over a small rolling hill flowing out into a football field–size meadow. Calling quietly to the others, I train my binoculars on the bear while a spotting scope and another set of binoculars are hastily pulled from nearby tents. All eyes focus across the Talkeetna to the rich, green field four hundred feet up the opposing mountainside. Over a slight rise lumbers a gargantuan, cinnamon-colored grizzly sow, with swagger to match. She's not alone. Three dark-colored cubs, ready to be fledged, come rollicking after her, chasing each other in the meadow. By all rights the cubs are full-grown bears, absolutely gigantic by standards in the lower forty-eight states. Having seen plenty of grizzlies in the wild, I can affirm these bears are supremely humongous.

This light colored female grizzly and her triplet cubs are foraging for roots, herbs, tubers, grasses and whatever else her sensitive nose can find. All summer long she has been teaching these little cubs the tricks of survival.

We're staring at the well-known and justifiably feared *Ursus arctos horribilis*, or inland grizzlies, cousins of the larger coastal Alaskan brown bear (*Ursus arctos*). Inland grizzlies tend to be smaller but a little more ferocious and confrontational than Alaskan brown bears. Speculation about this difference in temperament centers around food supply. Especially in the lower forty-eight states, inland grizzlies have less food, less habitat in which to roam, and hence, greater potential for run-ins with other grizzlies and humans.

Two words immediately come to mind as the gigantic sow struts across the meadow—Oso canella—cinnamon bear. It's hard for me to accept that she is so large, so massive. Compared to other grizzlies I've seen, even the stuffed trophy grizzly in Anchorage Airport's lobby, this bear is the true unit normal deviate, or the farthest statistical outlier on the bell-shaped curve. She's simply tremendous, without flab; all rippling fur and muscle. You would not want to meet her, much less any one of her cubs on the trail.

Undoubtedly they are heading down here to their feeding ground. It's their salmon- and berry-laden scat on which we trod; their droppings upon which our tents sit. I'm just thankful that we're looking at them across the Talkeetna River instead of on the edge of camp. What if we had run into them earlier when bushwhacking up the hill? That would have been a fatal confrontation—and I don't mean bear fatalities—because she has three feisty cubs to defend. There would have been total carnage. I don't care how good a shot Jim is with his intimidating buffalo gun. He can't shoot that fast or accurately.

Jaws drop as the bears amble down the meadow. We can't find words to express our wonder, excitement, or fear. It's so beautiful how they ripple along without a single care in the world. And then, the sow catches a scent of something—us?—and they scatter in the forest.

Gone. Just like that.

It's the end to a perfect day. We sleep sounder that night knowing they are up valley; silently hoping they have other blueberry and cranberry bushes that need tending, other side streams running full with fresh salmon, and that our good luck will continue to hold through the night.

Today we will float roughly twenty-five miles to the mouth of Devil's Canyon, and the following day, descend through eighteen miles of raucous white water. For the third day in a row we're blessed with good medicine in the form of bright sunny skies and only a few passing puffy clouds. Rafts push off and we settle into the mellowest morning imaginable while the guides do all the work, watching carefully for the deepest channels and benefiting from many eyes on five rafts. Our assignments are easy enough: First, watch for wildlife; and second, don't fall off the raft.

Eric Brown is guiding my raft. He not only has magnificent experience in the Alaskan wilderness, but also unbridled enthusiasm as well. He shares his fascinating knowledge about Alaskan mountains, animals, trees, fish, and birds—what an encyclopedia. But, during a moment of calm water when the Talkeetna simply flows quietly, he asks if we know the reputations

The bald eagle has staged a remarkable comeback since the banning of DDT. They have always been common in Alaska but now there are many nesting pairs in the lower forty eight states as well.

of our guides. When Eric told his guiding buddies over a frosty cool one in Talkeetna that he was rafting with Jim Hendrick and Bruce Helin, they didn't believe him. These guys are legends in the field, the absolute *best*, with reputations for leading professional rafting to its highest standard. Eric was learning the ropes from the crème de la crème.

Bald eagles are everywhere along the river, whether perched stoically on top of spruce trees, circling high overhead, or soaring low along the river. Immature eagles with brownish-tan and white mottled feathering are overly abundant, attesting to the Talkeetna as sanctuary. You almost reach the point of being blasé; of thinking, "Ho hum, another eagle." In some respects they're like sparrows, until hitting a stretch of river where sightings diminish. Then you can't wait to see another.

Temperatures gradually warm up as the morning progresses, lulling us into deep calm, almost repose. Waves rhythmically slap the rubber rafts, gently rocking in cadence with the river's flow. Sun penetrates bone-deep. I realize that things have slowed down — there's no set destination or time to be there, no latté to crave, no competition from others in the workplace, no insults and little indignities. We've been out just long enough to have shucked off our former lives. Now we're in sync with the Talkeetna; on wilderness time.

Wilderness on a grand scale floats slowly by. Unnamed and scenic mountain ridges, spires, and peaks beckon us to explore. Crystal-clear creeks splash nosily into the Talkeetna, adding volume and power, and intriguing dark forest alcoves disappear from view — so tempting, calling us to investigate, full of adventure and grand surprises.

Our internal clocks are all screwed up. Time-zone changes and the sun's orientation have our bodies totally confused. Some are still wearing watches, but they have little relevance to our schedule. Consequently, when hunger finally sets in you are ravenous. Fortunately the guides are sensitive and beach the rafts accordingly.

We notice that bear and caribou tracks are everywhere as we unload the tables and supplies. The guides have this down pat — so seamless and efficient. The water filter is set up with a bucket, and hand-washing buckets and soap are placed in front of our tables where lunch is waiting.

Bears can be curious about what's happening in their territory. This is a sub-adult grizzly male.

There's no hemming and hawing out of polite manners or shyness. People take what they want, what they need, and seek out a quiet spot to contemplate the river. Then, in almost no time at all, we shove off and continue floating along with bloated stomachs filled to the brim.

Drifting late in the afternoon we swerve over to investigate a sparkling clear stream entering from a distant lake. The Talkeetna has progressively gained volume from innumerable tributaries along the way, but Prairie Creek, running thirty-five feet across, is substantial enough to fight off its glacial, silt-laden waters for many yards downstream, until the two eventually meld as one. Too-loó-uk guides whisper quiet innuendos about potential animal sightings on this special creek, a tributary normally laden with spawning salmon at summer's end. Beaching rafts on a cobblestone-covered beach, we clamber off looking forward to stretching legs, penetrating sunny warmth without the river's incessant flow of chilled air, and exciting explorations.

We are drawn to Prairie Creek, fascinated by its luminous water running fast and clear. Sunlight transforms rippling water into an infinite blanket of dazzling diamonds, water so pure and crystalline, it seems to be totally transparent. Round cobblestones pave this streambed in a perfect mixture of white, black, gold, brown, and blue-gray. Dark-green moss carpets some of the rock, evidence of nutrients from decaying salmon that gave their all to perpetuate their species. Narrow, rocky beaches keep the forest of birch and fir at bay, but only by a slim margin.

We carefully broach the forest's boundary after the guides inform us that once, on beaching their rafts, a curious grizzly suddenly walked out of the forest to investigate. Vigorously healthy trees shade underlying sun-thirsty vegetation and spongy forest floor—a forgiving mat of moss cushions every step, enabling us to walk noiselessly with Prairie Creek's incessant rumble muffling any sound. The crisp scent of forest draws us into a cool, embracing canopy where light evaporates, in sharp contrast to the glowing sunshine reflected off the creek's rolling waters.

Jim cautiously leads the way along a serpentine path beaten out of the forest by grizzly bears and rafters. Underbrush hides ferocious mega-

mammals at every turn—or so we think after seeing heaping piles of fresh bear scat laden with processed salmon. The path falls down an embankment and back up around a six-foot-high willow, giving ground to the recent high waters of Prairie Creek. Sultry air wafts up from the creek as hot sun briefly warms this bend in forest and river. Conversation so freely shared on the rafts tones down as we anticipate . . .

Our hearts pound a little harder.

Circling a copse of trees sloughed off in recent floods, forest is left behind for a

Ever wonder how many animals see us in the woods and we as human beings with our poor senses are completely unaware of them?

sixty-foot-long cobblestone beach littered with small branches and soggy vegetation. Jim hesitates, looking back to measure our progress, and I glance down on the gravel bar. A huge black eagle feather, one from the left wing's leading edge, lies at my feet—this must signify good luck.

Less than a minute later a brown grizzly appears twenty yards across Prairie Creek, headed straight for dense willows. We stop, quietly murmuring about the sighting. Did everyone see it? No problem; thirty seconds later the young grizzly strolls out of the willows searching for leftover salmon strewn along the beach. Suddenly it detects a scent and rises on hind legs, gazing in our direction and searching for the odor's source. Huge paws laced with razor-sharp claws dangle in front. It drops to the ground, hidden by five-foot-high willows, and fifteen seconds later, rears back up to test the air. A longer, more concerted gaze this time, and then the scent registers. But, which way will it go—toward us, as it has been traveling, or back into the bush? Good medicine holds as the grizzly retreats to the brush. We begin to breathe again, our pulses racing wildly.

AGGRESSION OR CURIOSITY?

When a bear stands up on its hind legs during an encounter with people, does that mean someone is about to become a quick deli meal; or, is the bear showing off its impressive stature; or, does the bear have another intention in mind?

Bears typically stand on their hind legs to gather more information through their senses—seeing, hearing, and smelling. Bears are generally not communicating aggression when they stand in such a fashion. However, information they receive and process by elevating their olfactory, optical, and auditory senses may lead to hostile behavior.

Bears have a phenomenal sense of smell that tends to dominate other senses. Precise estimates of grizzlies' ability to smell remain fuzzy. Recently, Dr. George Stevenson—a retired neurosurgeon in Jackson Hole,

Wyoming, who has been studying grizzly bear brains—concluded that their sense of smell is "thousands of times" better developed than humans (Chris Peterson, *Hungry Horse News*, August 3, 2005). It has also been suggested that grizzly bears can smell food some eighteen miles away (Dr. Dennis Casey; www.bearcountryusa.com), while polar bears are able to smell food ten miles away (The Virtual Zoo; http://library.thinkquest.org). Standing on their hind legs enables grizzlies to test the air by rising above vegetation and gaining greater exposure to scents being carried on the wind.

Bears may be able to hear almost as well as they smell. Rising up allows them to hear more clearly by removing obstacles that block, buffer, or reflect sound. In comparison, grizzly bears' eyesight is weak and closely approximates that of humans.

So, next time you run into a grizzly bear and it stands on its hind legs, keep your wits about you. Most likely it is only trying to ascertain what you are and whether you pose a potential threat. If the bear huffs, growls, snarls, or roars, then be prepared. It may charge. Flattened ears indicate aggression. Turning sideways may be an attempt to intimidate by showing off size. A standing bear is a curious bear, but standing may ultimately provide information that transforms curiosity into aggression.

After floating several more miles, a large sand-and-gravel beach beckons as our next campsite. The guides hit the current dead-on and, with a few muscles straining and some carefully placed oar strokes, swing us into a quiet eddy—an alcove formed by a dawdling side stream. Leaping off the rafts we begin to search for campsites. Grizzly bear tracks with deep claw marks extending well in front of each pad's depression carpet the beach. Even a diminutive paw print from a cub has signature gouges.

Half of our group huddles together in an informal tent city, circling the wagons and ensuring that any crazed bear intent on human flesh will be able to carry out its massacre with the greatest efficiency. I head off to the remotest fringe of beach fifty yards away across from a wide willow swath. I'm eyeing a site just beyond a wonderful five-foot round willow clump—modest screening from others.

. . . *What's that?*

Reaching the site I hear a deep, throaty growl and low roar lasting about thirty seconds coming from forty feet away in the willow swath. A bruin is in there and it's not at all happy to be bothered. Branches snap as it lumbers off, annoyed by the disturbance. Bears are as happy to avoid people in close encounters as we are to avoid them. They only seek the courtesy of not being surprised.

The fourth day of our trip dawns sunny yet again—certainly a record for Alaska. Everyone is jittery about the almost eighteen-mile stretch of Class III and IV white water in Devil's Canyon; for white-water junkies, the trip's apex. Bruce Helin serves as our guide this morning. Bruce and Nancy Helin own Professional River Outfitters in Flagstaff, Arizona, a firm that provides turnkey provisions to those drawing permits to raft the Colorado River through the Grand Canyon. Everything is provided— satellite phone, superb food allotted for each day, rafting gear, and so forth. The only thing they don't supply is common sense.

Bruce and Nancy, old friends of Julie and Jim, the owners of Too-loó-uk, flew their plane up to Talkeetna and then traveled along the river, scouting rapids. When Bruce tells us he has never rafted the Talkeetna before, a momentary twinge of concern arises. But, Eric's words keep resurfacing—these people are legends in their field.

Wet suits and dry suits are required protection from freezing glacial melt. While we're standing on the sunny beach, they're stifling. I ask Bruce which type of suit he thinks is best; he simply says that the guides will be wearing dry suits. What he doesn't say is that since we are sitting up front, all of the heavy splashes and waves will dowse us thoroughly.

Pretty clever. A last check is made of the campsite to make certain nothing is left behind, and then we shove off.

As we float for half an hour, the canyon gradually narrows and the Talkeetna's current becomes turbulent as water is forced into a narrower space. Riffles are more prevalent, only these have a menacing look compared to days earlier when braided channels dispersed the Talkeetna over a wider area. Rafts begin rocking a little more seriously and light laughter and conversation among rafters and guides have disappeared. Tension fills the air as we swelter along beneath sunny skies. Our drift is just fast enough so that cool breezes mitigate some of the stifling sensation that comes from being swaddled in all of that neoprene, coated nylon, Gore-Tex, and polypropylene.

Abruptly, rafts start pulling over to the side. We're last in our group and Bruce skillfully swings into what's left of an eddy already jam-packed with boats. Guides and rafters scale a steep, tree-covered rock cliff to scout the first three major-league rapids—Class IV+. The view is alarming. Any raft that can get through the dogleg canyon will surely be shredded in the waiting rock-garden rapids below.

A few last-minute adjustments before hours of serious white water demand our full concentration. In no time at all the guides are ready, and the fun—no fear—is about to begin. Jim's raft is the first to disappear down the dogleg and we watch as they're swallowed in dark mist, monstrous waves, and tortured rock walls. Shouts of glee—or is it desperation?—fill the air. After Nancy, we're next . . .

Just like that we're churning through a twisting canyon, dropping with an enormous flood of tan-white glacier water, clouds of mist, and chaotic waves slashing everywhere while Bruce keeps us off life-threatening boulders, whirlpools, and dangerous, dark currents. No sooner do we spin through the dogleg than a rock garden appears—literally in seconds—and it's dodging one fatal line after another over shouts of excitement as rafts wend their way through the maze.

And, just as suddenly as it began, it's over. Everyone makes it without any problem; without any close calls. We're flush with adrenaline and relieved that these renowned rapids are behind us, but if this is merely a sample of some sixteen miles more, it's going to be one long, bucking-bronco ride until we hit the barn. There's no large eddy in which to re-group, and the current is too fast for us to pull alongside each other to check things out, but it's plainly evident that we're ready for anything the river will throw at us. So, we relax a bit as the river straightens and a few serious riffles meld into a rapid float for the better part of a half-hour.

Bruce is just beaming, and the man of little words says just enough for us to understand that he had great fun—quite a compliment for the Tal-keetna, considering that he has run rivers all over the world. We can't see him in action as he is sitting behind us, but our peripheral vision catches him planting his legs for an impressive stroke this way or that, or for a se-ries of quick and powerful strokes to slip off a partially submerged boulder with torrent cascading over its bald head. More telling are the words spo-ken by oars and oarlocks, straining under the pressure of carefully placed strokes, and their cadence of groans while the raft is positioned just so for a sweeping chute of frothing white water.

A long stretch of wavy riffles leaves us wondering whether Devil's Canyon hasn't been oversold. Lulled into complacency with the ride, the sun feels good as it dries things out after our initial soaking. Bruce talks about his business and his incredible good fortune to have moments like this on new adventures. He's leading the life we all want to live.

Around a sweeping curve, the Talkeetna drops some six feet, with seri-ous rapids. Casual ease morphs back into focused attention as one string after another of jostling rapids looms ahead. We're twisting, turning, drop-ping into safe water after quickly slipping through chutes, bracing for a lit-tle carom off a stack of glistening wet boulders, and seeking quiet eddies after the wild stuff. Never does it seem like things are out of control. Bruce always hits it just right. His superior craft keeps the fun meter up there.

By the time we exit Devil's Canyon, everyone is ready for a break. A broad, sandy cobblestone beach waits for us, and as Bruce swings around, I jump off to secure the raft. After about five hours and eighteen miles, the white-water section is essentially over. Julie and Jim are unloading lunch supplies. The water purifier is set up and famished souls descend on the collapsible table. Lunch is exquisite.

We excitedly compare notes on the experience. There are no complaints, only elation about the wild ride. The adventure was beyond compare. We have rafted one of the world's greatest wild rivers—and lived to talk about it.

It's time to change into more relaxed gear now that the serious white water is all through for the day. Has it ever felt this great to take off wet clothes, replacing them with warm, dry comfortable pants and shirts? We're moving in slow motion, relishing the sun's warmth and feeling the glow of a majestic experience. Phenomenal weather continues, and while I'm changing my shirt I think about what it would be like to have had rainy weather on this trip, particularly now. Cold rain would really have turned up the shiver level a notch or two.

While others fiddle around with their gear, I head downriver about a hundred yards toward an unusual copse of birch and willow isolated from the main riverbank by about fifty feet—and then I see him.

At first it looks like a grizzly headed away from me, disappearing into the bush. But moments later it meanders out again, heading my way. It's a huge black bear—at least 400 pounds. My olive-green wind pants and sea-green shirt offer perfect camouflage against the birch and willow foreground. Since I've ducked a little to better conceal myself among the branches, this unsuspecting bear ambles along totally unaware of my presence, just seventy-five yards away.

Most of the time this bear has nose to ground, swaying back and forth among the willow bushes lining the river. It's apparently looking for dead salmon or drift beached at a high-water point. As it comes closer I realize why I thought it was a grizzly. This bear is super-fat with glistening black fur—even the bear's muzzle is richly black. Huge dinner-plate paws plop down with each step, totally ignoring the grapefruit-size river rock lining the channel. A trickle of sweat runs down my side while the bear comes closer, investigating its surroundings.

I have to make a decision; either I leave now to inform our group while the bear is poking around among the underbrush forty yards away, or I need to step out and give the bear plenty of time to recognize that I'm here.

Brown bears grow large on the abundant salmon along the coast of Alaska, in this case Katmai National Park. Inland bears have to work harder for their food and thus seem to be grouchier with intruders, whether they are other bears or human observers.

A curious young black bear in a field of orange hawkweed sniffs the air. It pays to be alert as the mother is sure to be somewhere close, and you don't want to get between a mother and her youngster!

It is fun to watch bear behavior. In this case, a two-year-old sleepy female cub will not nap unless she can be touching her sleeping brown bear mother.

There are a number of salmon fishing techniques employed by brown bears. It is thought that most are learned behaviors, passed on by their mothers. Here a bear is chasing down salmon using speed. In short bursts a bear can run faster than a racehorse.

After coming out of hibernation bears are still lethargic and rest often. This young subadult has found a nice spot on a ridgeline for a daybed. His winter den site may have been in one of the background snowfields.

It's a traumatic adjustment for the second- and third- year cubs when their mother aggressively chases them off. They are now on their own for the first time in their lives. The siblings will often spend the summer and fall together, and may even den together in the coming winter.

A young grizzly cub. Cubs are often born with a white bib around the neck and shoulders; this coloration usually disappears as the fall coat grows in. Like a human infant, this cub appears to be sucking on his paw.

A real fishing specialist—this brown bear has found a deeper hole in the salmon stream and dives under water to catch his meal. Here, he is coming up for a breath of air.

Spectacular mountain scenery is part of bear habitat in Alaska. In late May, June, and July males are constantly on the lookout for receptive females during the mating season. In this case a mature female is on the move with two suitors following just out of sight.

A black bear mother and cub. Black bears can come in a number of different colorations including brown, cinnamon, and even white! Notice that this black colored parent has a brown colored youngster.

This had the makings of a very dangerous confrontation in Glacier National Park, Montana. In areas of thick vegetation along hiking trails it is important that the bear is forewarned that humans are in the area. Loud talking, bear bells, and large groups are the keys to safety in bear country.

Generally we think of grizzlies as creatures of the deep dark forest. Prior to white man invading the west, these bears were animals of the open plains.

I don't want to surprise this massive bruin at the last minute. Undetected, I move quickly back to tell our group so they can enjoy the experience too. The bear keeps lumbering along, looking for a morsel or two. Now it's twenty-five yards away and I'm beginning to wonder what kind of confrontation waits.

At the last moment, the great black bear startles. Its head swings out of the underbrush and for the first time I can clearly see its broad face. Ears pivot forward while the bear's snout rises three inches, testing the air. Beady, coal-black eyes squint to decipher unusual, multihued shapes. In my peripheral vision everyone is standing dead still. While no one moves a muscle, I can hear a couple of deep swallows and several panting breaths as our group tries to cope with this omnivore's up-close-and-personal presence. A little zephyr blows past carrying the smell of acrid perspiration and anxiety that even I can detect without a bear's fine olfactory ability.

One quick scent by the bear and it's headed to higher ground—crashing through the underbrush like a stampeding elephant. A loud, collective sigh, similar to a large hot-air balloon suddenly deflating, spills out as we express our relief. In its wake is spontaneous frenzied babbling about this bear and how close it came. If any of our group is using the woods at this moment, they will never forget watching the bear whiz by them, scrambling to get away. What an unbelievably great way to cap off a perfect day's adventure.

All good things must come to an end, and on the fifth day our float will be finished. The "monotony" of yet another sunny Alaskan day greets us, and by the time it's over a new high temperature will be set in Anchorage. We drift along, a pleasant day with sightings of humongous black bears and bald eagles soaring overhead. The black bears are usually a quarter- or half-mile up various side channels where small streams flow into the Talkeetna. They're close enough for us to recognize that they aren't grizzlies but too far distant for meaningful interaction. Most are too busy pawing away at salmon carcasses rotting along the beaches to even register that we're floating by.

At this point the Talkeetna is easily a half-mile wide in spots, with long, narrow islands cleaving it into several channels. Because the river is approaching an almost perfectly flat floodplain merging with the Susitna, the Talkeetna spreads, maintaining only a smidgen of current.

Eventually, increasing sightings of homes on the river's bank begin to chip away at the feeling of wildness. Then comes a flotilla of jet boats carrying sightseers with the promise of wildlife viewing.

A close-up view of a grizzly bear standing on its hind legs is one of the most awesome sights in nature. You know at that time you are in the presence of animal royalty!

Late in the afternoon the take-out point arrives. We feel like french fries from the blistering sun, but nary a gripe is heard. It was a trip of a lifetime; an adventure beyond imagination. Whether the Talkeetna River, Devil's Canyon, vast forests bracketing the river, high mountain peaks of the Talkeetna Range, abundant wildlife, or, Oso canella, Alaska delivers incredible summer adventure and unbridled, adrenaline-laced moments.

6

SEARCHING FOR GRIZZLIES IN THE CANADIAN ROCKIES

The Canadian Highway winds gently along milky-white Bow River, which in the beginning of July roils relentlessly downstream—an unstoppable mass—the product of very heavy runoff from winter snow and glacial ice. It's like returning home after a long absence with impenetrable fir forests, bountiful freshets dropping from mountain spires, and sparkling green grasses in open areas enticing wary elk, moose, and bear. Lingering gray-white snowfields in their final crystalline days wait to repeat the ageless recycling of precipitation. Looming shale, gneiss, and granite peaks call with adventure while massive blue-white glaciers tucked back in the farthest cirques lounge luxuriously on northern slopes.

Grizzly bear over-crossings appear along the highway. Mimicking the natural environment, these concrete-based bridges landscaped in soil, rock, trees, and shrubby vegetation form overpasses for migrating bears. Some limited success has been reported in encouraging grizzlies to migrate across the Bow Valley to access seasonal vegetation.

Less than an hour from Banff, Moraine Lake huddles beneath the Valley of the Ten Peaks. A scene formerly etched on Canadian twenty-dollar bills, it's truly an impressive sight—better than its cousin, Lake Louise, one substantial ridge to the north. Ringed by glaciated peaks, Moraine Lake holds enchanting jade waters from minute glacial silt suspended in streams and rivulets. Most people see this sight after a thirty-minute

Moraine Lake in the Valley of the Ten Peaks is one of the most scenic landscapes in the Canadian Rockies. It's also prime bear habitat!

stopover by bus, recreational vehicle, or car—another pretty sight to be photographed. But the most stunning scenery is found trailside above the tree line.

As dusk falls over the mountains it's a perfect time to get out and find wildlife. Binoculars in hand, I search in vain for moose and elk in the valleys before strolling around Moraine Lake. A slight drizzle adds perfect counterpoint to wet wilderness looming above, waiting for me until the next morning. How refreshing to have water falling, floating, easing down from gray and darkening skies. At any other moment I would have cursed this intrusion; however, tonight sleep will come quickly in the silence of softly breathing forest and the tension of active glaciers overlooking Moraine Lake.

A well-used, almost trampled, trail at the west end of Moraine Lake switchbacks steeply into alpine country. My plan is to reach this high country very early tomorrow—sneak up on any grizzly bears that might be foraging on high, lush avalanche slopes and tarn-filled meadows resplendent in summer flowers. If not grizzlies, then perhaps shaggy-white mountain goats will be lower on the mountain due to clouds, wind, and rain.

There's no adventure quite like being the first up this trail in early morning, winding through blind alleys of stunted fir, vigilantly alert for the great bear—pulse racing, breathing hard, anticipating a confrontation around the numerous hidden bends, and pepper spray set to go.

More often than not I come away empty-handed, but that doesn't matter. It's all about feeling alive; a tingle going down my spine at each sharp turn in the trail, lungs aching from almost jogging uphill, and face being slapped by the cold. In the inevitable early-morning frost, I'm blowing out clouds of fog while hoofing it as fast as I can go. Wooden bridges crossing tiny creeks are coated with an unblemished ultrathin layer of sparkling white ice crystals, so I know that I'm the first to come this far—that's why I've worked so hard to get here. It's the thrill of the unknown. Easing out of the subalpine forest into a massive meadow with sparsely scattered trees is terrifically exciting.

Unfortunately, next morning it's raining persistently and our cabin won't release me. Snug at home, remembering too many mornings where creature comforts were sacrificed in favor of the trail, I burrow back into bed with a good book, the heater gently creaking and crackling with warming, shimmering waves. Life is good; adventure can wait.

Banff, Moraine Lake, and Lake Louise are merely eye candy compared to Lake O'Hara, directly west across the Continental Divide. A private inholding, Lake O'Hara Lodge sits alongside an incredible subalpine lake with towering rock peaks, cirques, and glaciers soaring above. Under strict oversight by Parks Canada, only a limited number of people are allowed to stay at the lodge and its cabins, in a fabulous campground, or at the Elizabeth Parker and Abbot Pass huts/chalets maintained by the Alpine Club of Canada. A quota system keeps the number of visitors down and consequently minimizes environmental degradation and encroachment on grizzly habitat. East of the divide—Lake Louise—is like Grand Central Station; west of the divide—Lake O'Hara—is like heaven.

Valerie and I catch a bus into Lake O'Hara that afternoon because no cars are permitted on this forest road. The Lodge provides occasional shuttles for guests and campers. After settling into our cabin we head to a Craftsman-era lodge complete with dining room. Over dinner guests share the thrilling news that trails at Moraine Lake were closed this morning due to a mother grizzly and her two cubs. I'm astounded; profoundly disappointed because my preference for a little comfort caused me to miss an encounter of the furry kind. If I had only gone for a little walk in the rain I might have encountered the Rocky Mountain's magical talisman.

Assigned to a little cabin on Lake O'Hara's shore, we begin roughing it, luxury-style. From the cabin's porch, a pristine wilderness tableau unfolds in the gathering dusk; impressive snow-covered and rocky peaks surround the lake. Except for the gentle lapping of water on a pebble-strewn shore, almost no noise is detectable, only the sighing of a vast and ultimate wilderness. Inside the tiny log cabin, spare as can be, silence is relished. Thus begins one of those very rare experiences where absolutely everything is perfect. Lake O'Hara Lodge provides excellent cuisine and service beyond the highest expectations. But the food and lodging are only civilized distractions.

Lake O'Hara is all about world-class alpineering in the grand European tradition. Guests reserve sack lunches for backcountry adventures throughout the surrounding trail-woven mountains. Possibilities are endless. And after a long day of scrambling up this majestic peak or that; after wandering along the rock-strewn base of world-class cliffs; after picking our way through emerald larch-filled forests past sequestered black pools, azure tarns, and silent bogs; and after rejoicing in a land overflowing with crystalline water, we head back to the almost sinful creature comforts of a hot shower, fabulous food, and informative entertainment by local wardens. Alpineering definitely works for us.

We came searching for adventure and high precipitation and we've found both. A cold front passes through Yoho National Park resulting in sporadic icy rainsqualls, lots of blustery wind, and fast-falling frigid temperatures. At the cabin as we look out on wilderness raked by storms, gray-black clouds break chaotically enough to glass several avalanche slopes. High on an almost vertical couloir, long free of snow and nurturing abundant green vegetation amid crevices and table-size boulders, two ghostly white forms move circuitously in the alpine gardens. A mountain goat and her kid are seeking morsels among steep boulder faces.

Many folks visit the Canadian Rockies just hoping for a glimpse of a grizzly (from the safety of a vehicle)!

Unfortunately the clouds fail to rise off expansive rock faces and cliffs toward the west where grizzlies frequent McArthur Pass. This isn't very good weather for alpineering or searching for bears unless you enjoy getting extremely cold and wet, clawing your way up peaks only to see nothing but clouds two feet in front of you.

The Odaray Highline Trail to these choice ramparts is under voluntary restrictions due to grizzly bears preying on mountain goats that have fallen from dizzying heights. The trail crosses a migration route used by grizzlies over the eons; bare spots in mountain soil are formed when each bear steps precisely in the same footsteps as its predecessors. This is part of the allure in coming to Lake O'Hara—access to grizzly bear habitat and phenomenal alpine country.

Down by Lake O'Hara, in Le Relais Day Shelter, a research study describes frequent encounters between humans and grizzlies in this area around 9:00 A.M. during the summer months. When the first inbound bus of the day pulled up to the shelter and disgorged its load, the strongest hikers racing toward the cliffs were inadvertently the first to come across grizzlies feasting on recent mountain goat kills. Inevitably several maulings resulted from this unfortunate intersection of bears and hikers. Wisely the Park Service moved the trail a mere one hundred meters and confrontations decreased dramatically.

By now we've had more than our desired share of persistent rain. As if reading our minds, it suddenly stops and the clouds part, letting sun flood our rocky subalpine basin with an ethereal, golden glow. Folk at the lodge tumble out of their rooms destined for frigid high peaks and distant ice-covered lakes. My target of choice is McArthur Lake because I want to look down into the measureless reaches of McArthur Valley where flawless grizzly habitat waits.

Through stunted fir trees in a vast, rock-filled meadow our trail heads upward. The air is bitingly fresh now that cloud cover has been lost. Mixed in is the dank smell of rich earth exhaling from constant moisture. The world sparkles as raindrops perch precariously on the ends of fir branches, waiting for that moment when gravity, wind, and hydraulic accumulation combine to commit their final fall. Latent clouds scuttle past, raising the question of how long this vivid sunshine will last.

Along a football field–size avalanche slope of sharp-edged, black-gray boulders shaped like chaotic cantaloupes, an almost imperceptible trail switchbacks toward higher peaks. This alluvial rock slope is bordered by a forest of gigantic larch trees whose needles turn a brilliant mustard-gold before being shed each year. Slick from rain, the rock slope has been invaded by dark-green moss and lichen. Since everything is wet, it's difficult to distinguish where to go in this scree field. Fortunately each switchback begins at the edge of forest amid boot-beaten soil and heather where others have pivoted toward the spires. Climbing higher up the mountainside, it's not very long until snowbanks make progress over the scree piles dubious.

Adrenaline goes up a notch.

Lost in a dense copse of trees, the trail is merely a reflection of what previous visitors gauged to be the most direct path toward small Schäffer Lake. However, on a two-foot base of icy snow, the path is a bit more decipherable than the scree pile. Warm from the waist up thanks to the penetrating sun, and cold from the waist down thanks to the refrigerating effect of snowbanks, a gust of wind brings descending wisps of cloud and speculation that harsh conditions are returning. It would be a long trek back down to the lodge in chilly rain on an obscure path—prime ingredients for disaster.

Adrenaline goes up another notch.

The pendulum swings back in the other direction as our trail descends for one hundred yards while the sky clears and wind abates. From fright to fancy, the theater opens on a beautiful shallow lake reflecting rocky peaks overhead. In this part of the world it might be viewed as just another insignificant lake, but here in a pass be-

Mountain goats share habitat with grizzlies and black bears in the Canadian Rockies. In the spring bears scavenge on the carcasses left after winter avalanches.

tween legendary mountains, Schäffer Lake is much more. You can read the harsh Canadian winter in its depth, countless migrations of grizzly bears on its shoulder each year as they seek access to goaty morsels, and lushness where glorious wildflowers and vivid blossoms herald in a fleeting summer along Cataract Brook.

At McArthur Pass marginal weather raises the question of how much farther to go. We're on the edge of the grizzly zone looking down into the stupendous valley through which McArthur Creek flows. Parks Canada has closed this trail to maintain grizzly habitat. But the Park Service can't control grizzlies who wander up this valley to where we're now standing on their way to the base of sheer cliffs above to scavenge carrion, or toward verdant vegetation in the drainages of Morning Glory and Duchesnay Creeks.

They're out there . . . somewhere.

Out come the binoculars. It's amazing what simply being still for a few moments can do for seeing wildlife. When we move through a forest or across a mountain—with or without stealth—animals tend to adjust accordingly. They seek cover and end vocalizations until we are well past. The probability of sightings increases as we hunker down and blend in with our surroundings. That's what we're doing now at the base of several conifers, but nothing shows. Eventually cold wind rousts us from our lair and mission to find grizzlies. Today the price of cold weather is just too high to sit still for very long.

Our alpine ascent done for the day, the way back is all steeply downhill. Keeping a close eye on the trail ahead is no problem, but visions—hopes—of a grizzly sighting periodically flash across my mind. There's no reliable way to predict where the bears will be sighted. However, I'm coming to realize that the best food sources are probably thousands of feet lower in the river valleys where gathering summer warmth has already produced thick green grasses and edible blossoms.

Veteran hikers in the Canadian Rockies give grizzly bears great respect. Chris Townsend, who chronicled a hike the length of the Canadian Rockies in his book, *High Summer*, reported on bear activities at Lake O'Hara in the course of his walk:

> During the six-mile, 2,400-foot climb [to McArthur Pass] I found fresh bear droppings on the trail. With no signs or warnings I hadn't given bears much thought in recent days but suddenly I found myself anxiously surveying the avalanche slopes I was crossing for any movement. Near the pass a warden, on foot for once, greeted me. The first thing Alan Knowles, the Lake O'Hara warden, as I later discovered he was, mentioned was the bear sign. Had I seen any grizzlies?

Townsend goes on to mention that three grizzlies were active in the very drainage through which I am now walking.

Adrenaline up yet another notch.

Clouds swirl up around the peaks during our descent on mountain trail swamped with tiny rivulets splashing down an ever-changing course around rock and root. The temperature continues to fall as this storm blows through, leaving partially cloudy skies and prospects for clear days in the future. One thing is certain: The monotony of the same weather day in and day out is not going to be a problem on this trip. Variety is becoming the spice of life.

Next morning a popular trail leading several hundred feet up to a vast granite table, the Opabin Plateau, is opened by the park warden. This plateau is a broad slab of delicate subalpine country laced with tarns and lakes surrounded by rocky shores at the feet of glaciated slopes. Despite a frigid morning it seems like a great destination under the assumption that skies will remain clear and summer's warmth will replace the cold front that has moved through. Wearing virtually all of the clothes I've brought to Canada, the sooner the trail begins the climb to the plateau, the better to warm cold fingertips, nose, and ears. With my blood thinned from temperatures in the midnineties back home, it's tough to feel sufficiently warm in this achingly beautiful, but cold high country.

The trail climbs one hundred feet to serene Mary Lake at the base of Opabin Plateau. Early-morning sunlight dances on bobbing waters as slight breezes tease its surface. Reflections of regal, cloud-hidden peaks confirm that inclement weather is hanging on, but it doesn't dampen our optimism. We can stop right here and spend the entire day, the rest of the season, the remainder of our lives in this unbelievably stunning setting. Our senses are filled with incredible mountain splendor as we drunkenly rotate 360 degrees to take a visual reading.

The way to warmth is uphill out of mountain shadow and to the towering plateau. The trail switchbacks in earnest over scree piles recently freed from blanketing snow. Water gurgles everywhere, a delight and reaffirmation that our planet has not gone dry. Views to the north and grizzly terrain open rapidly. A quick survey through binoculars shows nary a soul nor bear on the vast mountain face. Thankful for an excuse to stop, we look above to an overhanging lip of the Opabin Plateau. Sun is shining up there and the sooner we reach it the better, as we don't have much faith in the conditions given the swirling clouds and deep-freeze temperatures.

A narrow gully defines the beginning of the end as a small stream burbles off the plateau and down the rock slide. Brightening sky and soaring, snow-covered peaks frame views south to Opabin Basin once over the lip. So this is what the commotion is all about; bordering between subalpine and true alpine country, the Opabin Plateau is the bed of a former glacier, a hanging valley filled with rock, water, and dwarf fir and larch.

The level plateau is truly enchanting. A trail weaves around waist-high boulders with gray-green fir and almost black heather nestled in crevices and on high spots free of plentiful water. An overflowing sense of purity penetrates the waters as light reflects off rock from clear depths of pools both shallow and deep. All of this beauty sits nestled between huge soaring cliffs rising to glaciers and mountains—Yukness, Lefroy, Glacier, Ringrose, Hungabee, Wenkchemna, Victoria, Schäffer—whose peaks are discreetly hidden in clouds. At this moment so many other

Mount Athabasca and Hilda Peak in the Canadian Rockies are just two of hundreds of beautiful peaks that bears call home.

stunning wild places appear rather commonplace and almost tawdry by comparison.

On slippery, smooth rock overlooking Lake O'Hara at the base of Opabin Plateau and grizzly country to the northwest, I rummage through my pack for a small bunch of sage. I typically carry a sage bundle for meditative moments and to help send good thoughts on their way.

With frozen fingers I try to light the gray, leafy bundle, but erratic breezes are picking up and extinguishing the flame. In fact, small amounts of snow begin to fall slowly and luxuriously down from the heights. Looking up at the growing cascade, the sight is spellbinding. Golden light spreads through tattered clouds and softly falling snow, warming the plateau while belying the reality of frigid blasts from another season and another land. Just a few days before, I'd made my escape from too much sun, heat, and dryness; now it seems that winter is returning—the challenges of alpineering.

The sage initially refuses to light, but after several matches it glows weakly as flame transfers to leaf. Mountain spirits will have to be happy with a puff of scented smoke sent skyward. As a little curlicue rises from the sage, a strong zephyr from the west extinguishes it. Grabbing my pack and putting gloves back on, it's time to cross the plateau before weather worsens and the trail is further obscured—a trail that is already difficult to negotiate among rocks and latent snow.

Up a little ridge and down another and we're able to take the measure of Opabin Plateau. More than a bit anxious in view of the deteriorating weather, we're determined to find where the trail exits back down through the green, dark forest to Lake O'Hara below. Across a wide expanse of flowing water coming from two enchanted lakes—Hungabee and Opabin—to the south, we can see the trail over to the east. The beauty of this garden returns with a slam. It's so gorgeous; the Opabin Plateau almost takes our breath away. Vaporous, muted light is shining down on a wonderland.

Crossing the rushing creek, pure white with spray and froth flowing from the higher lake basins, we jump to the other side and the trail destined to lead us to what now seems like relatively common, mundane Lake

This grizzly bear has just recently emerged from its winter den and is enjoying playing in the spring snow.

O'Hara. Falling snow increases, filtering the golden sunlight and adding urgency to the moment. Now certain of the way off the plateau, we amble along for several yards toward an immense cascade that culminates in a narrow waterfall. It is one of the most scenic and breathtaking sights we've ever had the privilege to behold. Swiftly flowing waters spread out to blanket the rock on their final moments at Opabin Plateau before dashing in a frothing crescendo over the plateau's lip, down the Opabin Cascades.

Looking back provides a magical moment that we all dream about; Opabin Plateau becomes a pristine garden. Shallow waters sparkle like a million gems in vanishing sunlight. Cream-colored rock with hues of brown, burnt orange, black, and green is visible under the waters, rendered as a kaleidoscope by fading sunlight. The golden aura of filtered sun and chaotic gray-black clouds slowly begins to dissolve as more potent weather descends on the alpine bowl, bringing wind-whipped snow. For a very brief moment we're treated to wildness beyond compare—a walk in the hall of a mountain king. Pulses racing, with one final glance back to savor the gift, we drop down into forest toward a fairy-tale land for mere mortals.

The next morning it's time to depart Lake O'Hara. Throughout the night I worry about the prospects of serious snow preventing our return to sunnier climes. On waking I glance out the cabin to check out the conditions.

Thankfully the snow level is about one hundred feet above Lake O'Hara. I relax a bit and finish packing. Then, just thirty minutes before departure, snow starts to fall in earnest at the lake. Gigantic potato-chip snowflakes deluge the lodge and cabins. After all, it is the first of July. Later that day we will return to midninety-degree temperatures and a lingering drought, but our minds will never relinquish the glory of a land where summer is more theory than reality.

As I look back on this adventure, it occurs to me how enjoyable European-style alpineering can be. At several points—slippery scree, grizzly bear haunts, snow-choked trails, descending through a snowy blizzard—we walked a razor edge toward possible danger, which made our hearts pump a little faster than normal. We didn't succumb to exposure or surprise a grizzly in a copse of stunted larch, but we did enjoy wilderness adventuring at its most civilized level.

7 ⌒

WHERE'S BEAR?

We may crash and burn before drifting out into the Main Fork as lifeless chunks of bruised and battered meat, but Dave Mills, owner of Boise-based Rocky Mountain River Tours, is precisely the sort of guide I want rowing my raft down the Middle Fork of the Salmon.

Dave does a fabulous job of selling the Middle Fork as the ultimate white-water rafting trip. He's a fanatic about the river's health and its conservation, and despite running the same river across the seasons, year in and year out, he continues to be fascinated by its grandeur and life-threatening thrill. Dave has promised big, humongous, water that is colder than ice cubes. Time to check the gear racks at home because this adventure is totally beyond the ragged edge of civilization. It will be one hundred miles through vastly remote country—Idaho's Frank Church-River of No Return Wilderness—that's just exiting from a long winter's sleep.

In truth, Dave and his wife, Sheila, represent the finest pair of ambassadors for professional rafting. They are passionately and obsessively dedicated to safety, guest service, and phenomenal wilderness experiences. Sheila makes certain that the menu is beyond reproach whether it's breakfast, lunch, or dinner. They both nurture a cadre of highly experienced, savvy, interesting, and informed guides. At their summer digs in Salmon, Idaho, Sheila and Dave maintain a warehouse of rafting gear complete with bunk quarters for their guides. The courtesy of a convenient crash pad is indicative of what the Millses believe is essential for solidifying the Rocky Mountain River Tours family. It must work because their guides only speak with the greatest respect for the proprietors.

Sheila and Dave have a rich history of guiding on the Middle Fork. They know every rapid and the fine nuances associated with each swirling challenge as seasons come and go. Not surprisingly, Sheila and Dave attract an international clientele. Dave boasts that former president Bill Clinton called up Rocky Mountain River Tours to schedule a run during his visit to Yellowstone National Park. The president called a little too late as the trip was completely booked. He had to go elsewhere.

June was still many weeks away and Dave assured me that he would be back in touch as launch time drew near. He shared the reality that late May and early June can be quite hairy out on the Middle Fork depending on runoff. But we knew recent winters were mild in Idaho, and serious melt-off had been under way for several weeks. There would be big water, but not disastrous water. That knowledge was reassuring.

Mid-morning of the launch day, after a one-hour bus ride from Stanley, Idaho, we pull up to Boundary Creek deep in wilderness forest. The guides are waiting impatiently. We are a bit late in leaving because one of the guests wanted to sleep in. But it's really not going to matter because somehow another outfitter has ripped off one of Rocky Mountain Tours' personal flotation devices. With one life vest missing, Tim, the lead guide, uses a satellite phone to call Stanley, Idaho, for a replacement. In the meantime, we go through a safety drill.

Even if you have run numerous rivers, and especially watercourses this challenging, you always pay close attention to the safety drill. This is a significant team meeting in which the playing field is leveled. Our lives could depend on what we do and how we react should we be unceremoniously dumped into the crashing, bubbling, frothing, and chilly Middle Fork. The fact that we will see plenty of Class III to Class IV+ water tends to intensify our listening skills. This is not just some downstream river; it's the Big Kahuna. People die on this trip.

Tom Brokaw's guided trip down the Middle Fork in 1970 turned into a nightmare beyond his wildest beliefs. Six people died that year on the main Salmon and Middle Fork when melting late-spring snow flooded the rivers. Brokaw's party lost a guide, Gene Teague, and a good friend— Ellis Harmon, a California lawyer and Sierra Club advocate. Lead guide Everett Spaulding had chosen a 16-foot rubber raft and two 16-foot McKenzie rowboats to negotiate the high water. They crashed-and-burned at Weber Falls. Miscues surrounding professional safety measures contributed to the deaths, including failure to wear life jackets and the unavailability of throw lines. As a result of this incident, by the mid-1970s the Forest Service had instituted policies regulating rafting on the Middle Fork.

Actually, the odds for a safe trip are remarkably in our favor. Twelve guests and seven guides are joining this float, three of whom are in training. We have five oar-powered rafts, two of which serve as support barges, and one twelve-foot paddle raft. This is an atypical guest-to-guide ratio, but we'll take it. It just means more experienced eyes to read the river.

Launch point is rife with colorful blue, red, and yellow rafts bobbing in the backwater, as well as a few kayaks. Sun beats away the chill and a more perfect day is hard to imagine. People are scurrying everywhere in an effort to get under way. A permit system controls use, and a Forest Service guard station sits just above put-in. Except for this bustling port of debarkation, there is seldom a sense of too many people out on the river in early season. Actually, a little company adds a false sense of security to the whole thing.

Todd Bradford introduces himself as our guide. He seems to be a friendly, yet serious, fellow paying close attention to how things are positioned on his raft. Todd concentrates on mentally going through the list of things he doesn't want to leave behind. And then he's ready; red life-jacket zipped tight and hands on oars.

Out of curiosity I ask what will become a very significant question: How many times has Todd rafted the Middle Fork? I'm anxious and really don't know what to expect. If someone has rafted this river ten to fifteen times, then perhaps they pretty much know what to expect.

Granted, it's a totally new run every single time. Water flow constantly changes over the course of one hundred miles as side streams ebb and flow. Massive thunderstorms in side canyons bring gravel, boulders, trees, and brush, creating new rapids. Seasonal variations come into play. Especially after winter's melt-off the first run can be very surprising, with big changes anticipated. Todd emphasizes that the flow will be higher this week compared to last week since recent snow in the high country is rapidly melting.

I'm a little astonished when Todd recounts sixty guided trips down the Middle Fork. That's pretty impressive. He's seen this river at some of its lowest ebbs and highest points. Best yet, he's here to talk about it. And as I get ready to ask Todd another pesky question, we push off into the forceful Middle Fork.

We're off . . .

Todd is constantly moving the oars as we juke around several water-shrouded boulders and bounce off projecting rocks. Then we spin around as he prepares for First Bend Rapid and an almost two-foot drop with a sluice of pounding, rushing white water. Thus begins the graceful dance of floating down a world-class river.

Todd lets us know that a major-league rapid, Class IV Velvet Falls, lies around the next bend. A prelude of riffles has us bobbing and careening just above the falls. Todd rows frantically, trying to stay left and heading toward a freight car–size boulder before slipping onto a glassy tongue of water that plunges precipitously into a churning pool and more riffles. Velvet Falls is a marvelous plummet amid wild spray and clawing boulders. As we exit into swift, tumbling cascades, all rafts score perfect rides. No calamities; just pure, unadulterated white water.

Floating along after Velvet Falls, we have time to enjoy the scenery. The Middle Fork's coniferous forest is strikingly wild and healthy. With the canyon's steep forested sides, and few beaches along the riverbanks, we're truly held captive by the Middle Fork. This is a phenomenal watercourse designated as a Wild and Scenic River thereby prohibiting the federal government from building major diversions or hydroelectric dams.

It's a long, long way to help should we need it. Except for several airstrips on private land, no plane can land in this tortured canyon, and even points where a helicopter can set down are few and far between. Hiking really isn't an option as trailheads are twenty to thirty miles distant. A satellite phone may provide contact, but we still would have to carry an injured person to a point where mechanized transportation could navigate. This is the reality of the Middle Fork; part of the price you pay for adventure.

River otters are always fun to encounter when hiking along mountain streams and rivers. Because of their curiosity they will often approach just to see what you are up to.

Normally I would be hanging onto the edge of my seat at every bend in the river, hoping to see a grizzly fishing for salmon. It seems implausible, but here in the middle of the 5,500-square-mile Frank Church-River of No Return Wilderness, there are no grizzlies. Without protection, the bears disappeared just before 1950. Wolves that also were extirpated have recently been reintroduced. They are now thriving in this vast ecosystem after finding deer, elk, sheep, and goats to sustain and expand their packs. Wolves have dispersed within this wilderness and the Selway-Bitterroot Wilderness.

Surprisingly, the Selway-Bitterroot and the Frank Church-River of No Return Wildernesses offer suitable habitat for grizzly bears even with diminished salmon runs. Normally these mountains receive exceptional snowfalls conducive to hibernation and winter denning by grizzlies.

Bears are strong swimmers and have no problem jumping in and swimming streams, rivers, and lakes.

Habitat destruction didn't lead to their decline; relentless hunting and lack of legal protection killed the last bear. Improved fisheries with abundant salmon would increase the probability that grizzlies could sustain a population of somewhere from two hundred to four hundred bears. However, there is sufficient large prey (deer, elk, goats, and sheep), small prey (marmots, ground squirrels, and chipmunks), and berry crops (huckleberries) to ensure the survival of grizzlies even without more salmon.

Shortly, the guides set up for The Chutes, Class III+, followed by Elkhorn Rapid. Powerhouse Rapids, another Class IV ride in this frothing high water, waits three miles downstream. Three drops have to be negotiated, as well as a shift in current that drives rafts against an imposing cliff. Todd becomes a little disoriented as we plunge into the second pool headed for a flip, but places an oar just in time for the current to spin us around again as we make the final drop.

Later in the afternoon Todd cautions about approaching Pistol Creek Rapid (Class IV), which is complicated by a microburst far upstream. So much debris, boulders, and gravel have swept down into the Middle Fork that the rapid has grown into a monster. Rafts pull together in anticipation, eyes strain to read the line of this tight, serpentine "S" switchback. Todd starts right, then caroms left toward a big hole before rowing frenetically to the right to miss Pistol Creek's cliff. We flop down the powerful sluice backwards—not exactly the way he intended—but upright, and spinning into a waiting eddy.

A mile and a half downriver is Airplane Camp, our home for the night—a huge bench sitting thirty to fifty feet above the Middle Fork, complete with towering ponderosa pines and comfortable needle-strewn flats. We've dropped a thousand feet over twenty-five miles since Boundary Creek.

By the next morning the river has risen a foot. Today will primarily be a float day with Class II water and an occasional Class III+ —Marble Creek and Jackass Rapids. Rocky Mountain River Tours' tradition is for guests to switch guides each day. Our guide today is Jim Norton, a biologist by training.

Norton is extremely passionate about restoring salmon to this watershed, and explains how the Snake and Salmon Rivers once flowed fully with salmon. Habitat destruction has rendered the Middle Fork almost salmon-less compared to a hundred years ago. That isn't progress. Norton shares his ideas about remediation, plans that are optimistic and big; plans that we need to embrace.

Jim and I are on common ground because his beloved salmon would add that extra margin to make reintroduction of grizzly bears a sure bet. We're not talking at cross-purposes—salmon versus grizzlies. In fact, we want the same thing—an ecosystem returned to its natural state. Unfortunately neither the salmon nor grizzly bear fared very well under the former Interior Secretary, Gale Norton. She stopped the citizen-run initiative to reintroduce grizzlies on public land in the remote Bitterroot Mountains, which includes the Frank Church-River of No Return Wilderness. She also proposed delisting grizzly bears as an endangered species.

DELISTING PROS AND CONS

When former Interior Secretary Gale Norton proposed delisting grizzly bears from the Endangered Species Act on November 15, 2005, she set off a wave of heated debate throughout the nation. The public had ninety days to comment on the proposed policy change. Strong opinions have been voiced both for and against delisting. A few of the key arguments are outlined below:

Pros

- Grizzly bear hunting could be reopened.
- Federal control of wildlife would be delegated to the state level.
- Grizzly bear populations are healthy and no longer need expensive federal oversight.
- Land and roads in mountains, forests, and rangeland closed to protect habitat could be reopened for other uses.
- Rules protecting bears will remain in effect in critical conservation areas and national parks.
- Grizzly bear population growth is so successful that increasingly large amounts of land need to be set aside to protect them. These lands are not available.

Cons

- There is confusion about jurisdictions (i.e., Primary Conservation Area versus Distinct Population Segment Boundaries), which will lead to unintended grizzly bear mortality.
- Endangered carnivores can only be considered viable candidates for delisting when prey species and food sources they rely on for sustenance are bulletproof.
- States where grizzly bears exist were ineffective in maintaining bear populations without the added protection of the Endangered Species Act.

- Motorized recreation continues to escalate without federal agency control, thereby jeopardizing suitable habitat.
- Logging, mineral extraction, and oil/gas extraction compromise habitat needed to maintain stable bear populations.
- Factions in Idaho, Wyoming, and Montana have historically been hostile to grizzlies. Delegating control to the state level will lead to population declines.
- U.S. Forest Service rules over intended grizzly bear protection have too much ambiguity.
- Once lands have been released from habitat protection, it will be difficult to secure these parcels if needed in the future.
- Grizzlies breed slowly and need more substantial protection. Relisting is cumbersome and slow.
- Poaching will increase.
- National parks will see their grizzly bear populations decline.
- Weak state budgets suggest they will have difficulty in managing the implications from grizzly bear delisting.

Whatever policy decision finally emerges, it is clear that unanimity will be very elusive. We do know that once a species is lost, it is gone for good. And, the belief that it's sufficient to simply have a few dozen survivors around to regenerate a population fails to consider the importance of diversity in the gene pool. California condors are a perfect analog. Although condors have made a remarkable recovery, genetic diversity has been compromised. These lessons should remain foremost in our minds.

Whatever decision is reached, we should remember that the U.S. would be considerably less of a nation without grizzly bears roaming wilderness areas in the lower forty-eight states.

Almost immediately after launching, a stiff upriver breeze begins blowing that shifts into swirling wind. This sends up lots of spray, dousing us and keeping Jim on his toes as he tries to avoid boulders and waves aggravated by the blowback. He also has more work to keep us moving forward since the wind is strong enough at times to almost halt our drift given the raft's protruding bow.

On the riverbank a trail paralleling the river is very distinct in spots, but disappears in others. Jim indicates that the Civilian Conservation Corps originally built the Middle Fork Trail, which the Forest Service continues to maintain. How they do this is a mystery, given the vertical rise of cliffs, rock avalanches, broad scree deposits, and undermining by the Middle Fork. In the full course of our trip we will only see one party of three people on horseback using the trail.

While we drop into an ever-steeper canyon below Cougar Creek Ranch at mile 40, the wind abates, the temperature rises, and a sense of magic drops like a cloak over the Middle Fork. Without any forewarning, we float into a caddis hatch.

It's as though a cloud has descended over the river. Caddisflies fill our eyes, mouths, and ears, but there's no escaping them. Jim is elated, fueled by the sheer abundance of life, cheering for the fishery he loves, hopeful that salmon are partaking in the banquet. The hatch goes on for about a mile and then slowly tapers off.

With a diminished fishery, the River of No Return is affected in often imperceptible ways. Bears prey on salmon and shed valuable nutrients through scat. This invigorates a fairly low nutrient environment. Salmon imply a more propitious habitat for birds of prey, especially for osprey and eagles. To this point, almost fifty miles downriver, we've only had occasional animal sightings. Given the vastness of this wilderness, we *should* be seeing more wildlife, but an important element—salmon in abundance—is missing.

Grizzly bears would add yet another dimension to the wilderness. Their presence would be entirely consistent with this great swath of wildland miles from urban centers. From a visitors' perspective, grizzlies would only improve the backcountry experience. Jim argues passionately

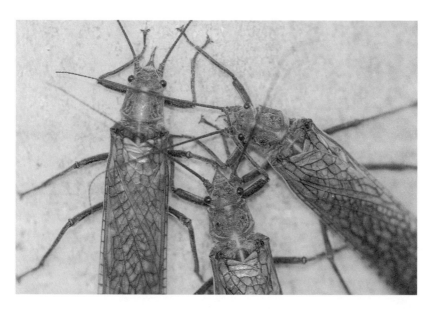

You know the fishing will be good when the stone fly hatch is going! Ugly they may be; trout nonetheless love them.

from a "pure ecosystem" standpoint that we need a healthy and whole wilderness. Without substantial grizzly or salmon populations, the ecosystem is severely compromised. His fervor is impressive—the sort of enthusiasm that we need to set things right—and we continue chewing on these thoughts throughout our float.

Late in the afternoon we approach Loon Creek, rushing into the Middle Fork. Camp perches on a scimitar of sandy beach and willows at the base of Simplot Ranch. A large green meadow serves as landing field and horse corral for a cabin huddled toward the hillside. A storm will come late at night delivering only a sprinkling of fat drops and plenty of wind. Loon Creek's headwaters must be in the storm's path because by morning it has risen half a foot and lost its crystalline character.

Next morning we shove off into the muddy, murky Middle Fork with Telly Evans at the helm. The float morphs into an almost continuous series of Class III rapids and plays out much like our ride with Jim Norton the day before. Plenty of thrills are sprinkled throughout this twenty-five-mile portion of the trip, but nothing serious enough to take us over the edge. It was simply a good day to raft and relax in a massive wilderness.

Camp is somber tonight. After seventy-five miles of rafting, we conclude tomorrow at the Middle Fork's confluence with the Main Fork. We're perched just outside the entrance to Impassable Canyon, so-called because no trail can negotiate the near-vertical cliffs. The canyon is literally impassable. This is the flashy focal point of a float trip down the Middle Fork; a treacherous ride through a steep canyon littered with serious rapids. If disasters occur, they tend to happen within Impassable Canyon.

It's an intimidating sight, with the massive river swollen to several times its size seventy-five miles upstream. We've got big water now; powerful flow that hates to yield to rough canyon walls. Frankly, it's more than a little unnerving to think that tomorrow we will try to ride this roller coaster to its conclusion.

We're having juicy steaks for dinner, embellished by tonight's educational session. Jim Norton is presenting a quick seminar on animal scat. Jim has formed a dung collection ranging from wolf to mountain lion scat. He discusses the various habitats and food sources each animal relies on for sustenance. The scat is a physical manifestation of the animals' varied diet.

Norton's scat collection obviously lacks one important sample—grizzly dung. However, its omission is a propitious point for campfire discussion about grizzly and wolf reintroduction. Several of us speculate on the value grizzlies would add to our wilderness float, even though the likelihood of seeing one of the great bears would be very remote. Simply having the possibility of seeing a grizzly bear is value enough.

Sated with fine food and wine, we wander off to bed; all are anticipating the big day to come. It has been a wild ride up to this point, but before long, this will seem like nothing more than child's play.

Breakfast is almost an afterthought. There's no kidding around, no casual conversation. We're on a mission, and everyone—guides and guests—know death potentially lurks down canyon. Will it be the guide standing next to me during rounds of hot chocolate and coffee that eats it big-time? Or will it be me?

We're past being anxious to get going, and as our group begins to load up I know exactly which guide I want to ride with—Todd. Although Rocky Mountain River Tours encourages guests to switch guides every day, you are free to select whichever guide you are most comfortable with for hairy sections of the river. If Todd can make it sixty times down this river, he can surely make it sixty-one. There's serenity in this knowledge as I clamber forward and settle in.

Two Class III rapids—Waterfall Creek and Big Creek—loom in sickening succession. Todd is more than ready and makes these warm-up rapids seem simple, but the Middle Fork is almost uncontrollably humongous by this point. A constant seething, rasping sound fills the air from too much water being forced through too little canyon. Quite frankly, the power of this river is frightening. All white-milk-chocolate, judging by the shoreline it's very deep, almost to the high point, as a matter of fact.

Todd's busy calling out the rapids to come: "We're coming up on Redside Rapid, Class IV+, and then Weber Rapids, Class IV." Our flotilla has drifted way to the right in anticipation of Redside's powerful tongue of frothing water that flows to the right, past a huge boulder dead center, and left of a towering rock on the right bank. Our raft suddenly picks up blinding speed, like being catapulted from a slingshot, before dropping down to the bottom of the rapid.

No time for adrenaline to seep out of our systems, as Weber Rapids waits a few minutes downstream. The line is dead center through a wavy rock garden. Todd shoots it straight and true, bouncing and jostling among protruding sofa-size boulders. Then, for the next five miles we break out into sun and a leisurely float. The Middle Fork is like this— pool, and drop over a hundred miles.

So goes twenty miles of life at the edge. No fear? That's not what I read in the faces and actions of guides or guests. Fear keeps us alive, cognizant of the fine nuances of canyon and river. Impassable Canyon contorts again and we negotiate several Class II and III rapids, almost child's play after Redside and Weber. Then Todd simply says, "The biggest, meanest rapids of the whole trip—Rubber Rapids—is just ahead. If you're going to take a swim, this will be it."

Lead guide Tim goes first. Two giant boulders pinch the river before it pours through a massive boulder-lined channel replete with six-foot whipping waves and bottomless holes. All eyes are on Tim as he swings a bit right and then plunges down, fires straight back up, shimmies sideways to the left a bit, corrects, and hits a wave train to victory. Well, almost. Mark, a guest, flips out into the water, half in and half out of the boat. His father is clawing desperately to haul him aboard. The call goes out— *Swimmer!*—but there's nothing we can do until this evil rapid has had its way with us.

Next are two female guides McCale and Keri who are rowing a support raft loaded with gear. They look spot-on-target—missing a plunging crash to the left bottom of the first hole and catching a series of bouncing six-foot waves—except for one thing. The wave train rises to an apex just as they exit the first major plunge, so they shoot skyward with the raft's bow scratching for the sun. What goes up must come down. When the raft bounces down, Keri—the guide who is rowing—is literally flipped right off her feet and into the drink. McCale scrambles to rescue Keri as the pilotless raft careens off huge waves.

We're next, with no more than fifteen seconds to prepare; then our raft rockets down the sluice channels headed for the colossal, frothing waves. We begin to slide left toward certain catastrophe when Todd digs in on the right side. We race to the top of the wave train a bit off kilter, and he drops an oar in exactly the right place because we straighten. Then the most beautiful thing happens.

We literally dance on top of the wave train as if each wave was intent on gently handing us off to the next. We barely bob from one wave crest to the next before it sets us down, oh so gently, in placid water.

It's over. Hissing water retreats, replaced by a placid chocolate flow. Now we scan for rescue assistance in front of us to prepare for others that follow. Our duty is well defined and we set up for the inevitable. The smaller paddle raft will assuredly not be able to dodge this bullet.

Jim Norton has had three examples to assess, and he barks the order to paddle full-on. He's straightened the tiny raft to mimic Todd's line. As they take the initial drop our hearts are in our throats. Here it comes. But this isn't just any set of river guides; this is Rocky Mountain River Tours. Norton absolutely, positively nails it. It's not as pretty as Todd's run, but it will more than do.

The Middle Fork settles down to a few more Class III rides that barely register on our fun meters. Ahead is the confluence with the Main Fork of the Salmon River. It's over; one hundred miles of excitement and life lived on the edge. As we lay back against

The wolf is reappearing in many parts of the west, due to natural recolonization and partly to do with reintroduction. Bears in Yellowstone National Park have capitalized on the wolf introduction by domineering wolf-killed carcasses. Such kills offer a source of high protein when they most need it after emerging from winter denning.

dry bags soaking up the sun, big smiles on our faces, spent from the rush of adrenaline, a single collective thought rises in unison.

Let's go again.

Rafting the Middle Fork of the Salmon River takes outdoor enthusiasts through one of the largest wilderness areas of the United States. Yet, is wilderness really wilderness when signature species such as salmon, wolf, and grizzly bear are virtually nonexistent, or extinct?

Grizzly bears, wolves, and salmon are native to Idaho and the Frank Church-River of No Return Wilderness. Both wolves and salmon endure in

One of the amazing sights in nature: salmon returning to their birthing freshwater stream to spawn and die.

this wilderness, but cling to life by the smallest margin due to human impacts on their environments. Grizzlies roamed this area until the late 1940s, and more than 1,200 continue to thrive east in the Greater Yellowstone area. That's a far cry from the 100,000 grizzly bears that inhabited this area two hundred years ago when Lewis and Clark made their epic voyage of discovery.

Make no mistake about it—the Middle Fork of the Salmon delivers awesome adventure in the form of a jagged-edge raft ride. However, how much more exhilarating would my journey have been if the fundamentally significant species—salmon, wolves, and grizzlies—were rife throughout the ecosystem? I don't necessarily need to see them on any given trip that I make to the Frank Church Wilderness. There's value enough in knowing that when I walk up a side canyon, I may startle a grizzly feeding on a mountain sheep carcass or a wolf trotting back to its pack.

Salmon, grizzly bears, and wolves all fit together to form a perfect whole. Human intervention hasn't improved wilderness; it's depreciated it and destroyed critical inherent interdependencies. Grizzlies simply need salmon in order to thrive. As has been observed in Yellowstone, grizzlies routinely prey on cutthroat trout (a salmonid) in streams; the same should hold true for the Middle Fork. Grizzlies also benefit from wolves due to their more efficient predation of ungulates, a lesson that has been learned a couple hundred miles east of the Frank Church Wilderness.

A rafting trip down the Middle Fork of the Salmon River is fantastic outdoor adventure. However, it pales in comparison to what might otherwise be possible if our society restored these vastly impressive wildlands to their original condition. It's not too late to make enlightened decisions that will nurture salmon, wolves, and grizzlies for future generations.

8 ℮∿

PASS IT ON

Thank God we're the first in our caravan.

Fat, dirty clouds roll thirty feet upward before hanging suspended above a rough, twisting gravel road. Beams of sunlight illuminate a concoction of tan and chalky white grit that will soon cover everything in sight. The clouds can ascend no higher, held in check by feathery limbs of monstrous Douglas fir and red cedar. Slowly the road's surface begins floating gently back to earth. Guerrilla plumes penetrate roadside shrubs, coating leaves with a smothering blanket. The Forest Service road undulates and curves, rocking us left to right through a green tunnel.

I'm beginning to wonder if this drive will ever end. How many hours have we been traveling, anyway? It seems like forever. Invariably trips like these result in ultimate, high-watermark adventures. Grand experiences have to be accumulated the old-fashioned way; you earn them. The hint of something extraordinary surfaces during interminable travel on the approach; when you conclude that it's better to turn around than to continue one pathetic second more. Patience will be rewarded, but that's little solace watching the better part of a glorious day slip away. Thousands of forested acres roll past the window, prime habitat for grizzly and black bear. Black-green subalpine lakes in rocky mountainous basins call distractingly. Wildflower tapestries covering alpine meadows lie in wait, peaking with a visual crescendo that no artist's canvas can possibly capture.

Firs whizzing by the car window reflect strobe-light flashes while thoughts drift to how deeply we've penetrated wilderness. My close friend and trail partner, Clio Thomas, has lived for years in the Pacific Northwest, and he certainly knows where and when to experience summer's climax—the Glacier Peak Wilderness. This time, however, it's beginning to appear that he's outdone himself. Only mature forest has accompanied us these last few miles. Thank goodness we haven't run into anyone else in this maze. Calamity is waiting around blind corners, narrow alleys, and widow makers—unforgiving tree trunks capable of stopping our car in its tracks. This is one time that wood breaks metal.

A clearing appears where the forest wanes, revealing a Forest Service campground. Even though it is high season, few tents or vehicles are observed as we blow by without slowing. Gad, how I love these campgrounds; gad, how I hate them. It's either feast or famine. Either everyone respects everyone else, or it's complete pandemonium—cackling adults, shrieking children, yapping dogs, musical bass beat thumping, doors slamming, engines revving. Typically, it's the latter. But, there's no substitute when friends huddle around a campfire sharing stories; bacon sizzles on the grill; and hot water for washing leaves you feeling like a million bucks. For a split second my mind wanders back to such memories, but I catch myself. None of that cushy luxury for us—we're bound for serious wilderness tonight, far from the comforts of car camping.

At the trailhead, boisterous teens tumble out of our cars filling the air with nonsensical chatter about this indignity or that; teasing the opposite sex; flirting in passive-aggressive ways; and, ruminating about how far they will leave the elders behind. It's all bravado designed to mask insecurities about being away from home and entering the foreign world of nature. Without cell phones, iPods, CD players, pagers, or PDAs, the prospects must be daunting—to confront wilderness bereft of those trusted lifelines. Apprehension is written all over their faces and posturing. They don't know what to expect, most of all about the potential for black and grizzly bears. They don't know the slightest thing about surviving out of the urban jungle. They cannot begin to fathom the physical challenges they are about to face. They don't know these things, because adults haven't taught them. *We haven't passed it on.*

After a half-hour of fiddling with this, exchanging that, and putting packs on and off about a dozen times, they set off, leaving a cloud of testosterone, unbridled ambition, subtextual fear, and furtive longing—the sorry angst of being teens. Clio will try to keep the more physically fit and rambunctious ones from unintentionally walking past our first campsite. Today it's my turn to ride rear guard. I'll sweep up any stragglers or misguided wanderers. Suddenly the parking lot is vastly empty and quiet.

Purposefully waiting ten minutes before launching, I hope they will more or less stay together. But, that's highly unlikely. Eventually some will grow tired and seek repose beneath skyscraper trees. Shade in cavernous glens provides a perfect remedy for drowsiness after a long ride. Others will become entranced by the rollicking White River flowing rapidly down its course. They'll be mesmerized, drawn by crystal-clear water and clean gravel beds alongside the trail. Excuses will surface about filling water bottles, but in truth, they're fascinated with the beauty of a mountain river—something far more interesting then lugging a heavy stone on their backs through hot sun.

Called to adventure, I slip on my gravity-seeking pack that's determined to pull me backwards—laid flat before even starting. Perhaps overloaded for this hike, it's too late now. Clio has the car keys and he's well up the trail shepherding lean greyhounds. Forty pounds settles around my midsection as reality hits home. I breathe deeply several times and then stop. It's so quiet; unnervingly so. Only a muted rush from the White River disturbs the invasive quiet. Not a single zephyr rustles the trees; only the breathing of wildness exhales through this stark gravel lot scraped out of virgin forest.

It's natural to think that the first fifteen minutes on a trail overflow with joy and wonder, but they typically unfold like the beginning of any other endeavor. First, there is the smothering sensation of an unexpected passenger on board—a cumbersome pack intruding on carefree movements. Next is a frontal assault by a rough wilderness trail. No longer bound to concrete and asphalt paths, your mind reprograms to cope with hidden depressions, unexpected roots, ill-placed rocks, malevolent branches, and assorted obstacles lying in wait for the unwary. Finally there is a futile attempt to take in the big picture of walking a wilderness valley while being flooded by smaller detail—an orange butterfly floating gracefully in dips and bounds downstream; sunlight flooding a lush thicket; a small grove of giant cedars across White River; a glimpse up to subalpine ridges; or, the trail disappearing among grasses and six-foot-high shrubs.

The prospects of a bear encounter are extremely high, and there is a distinct possibility that the bear might be a grizzly. From 1964 to 2004 there

have been twenty confirmed grizzly sightings in the North Cascades. It is believed that five to twenty grizzly bears live in this area, and that a reintroduction program could sustain a population of two to four hundred bears. But more importantly, one bear biologist confirmed a sighting of a grizzly bear on the south side of Glacier Peak in 1996—the very area we are now trying to wade through undetected.

Gliding along a valley floor in intense sun and high humidity from vegetation that has gone wild, we're becoming parched. White River is always to our left, south, about twenty

Young grizzlies are good tree climbers and it is only as they grow older that they lose that ability to conveniently climb trees. In the west there is a saying, "If you climb a tree to escape a bear and the bear climbs up after you, it's a black bear and if it just shakes you out of the tree, it's a grizzly."

to fifty yards away, obscured by impenetrable vegetation. Its whispering song is often audible, mocking us. Adding to this misery is the substantial mileage we've made over several hours as the trail begins to rise above the valley. Lush meadows near the river bottom are being left behind.

For the next several miles our trail winds through dramatically lush growth, so vigorous that the trail is completely covered. Even with our group having stomped through this dense jungle, it's difficult at times to decipher where to step. You literally have to push grasses and stalks of wildflowers aside to negotiate further. And, as you physically penetrate this living wall it occurs to you just how far civilization is being left behind. At least for this year the message is unmistakable—few have trod this fantastic valley. That raises the ante for bear encounters.

Keeping us on edge is a subconscious thought, progressively growing in my mind—this is optimum bear country. Water and feed abound. Hidden on the east slopes of the Cascades where more sun drives photosynthesis crazy and fewer visitors disrupt the tranquility of an extravagant buffet, this valley presents a perfect environment for bears. The problem is line of sight. With six-foot-high vegetation obscuring the trail, it's difficult enough to see the way, much less spot a bear. The unknown, but anticipated, sharpens a fine edge on my senses.

I pause to wonder whether I've missed anyone in this jungle. How would we explain that to nervous parents? Fortunately, ahead I can see that the valley ends, forming a more-than-mile-wide bowl, with an impressive rise toward the Cascade Crest. Entering a stand of rather spindly fir, runts in comparison with the monsters we left back in the valley's lower reaches, our group congregates in an opening south of trailside. They've found our camp for the night and packs are strewn about on the ground up against trees—ordered chaos.

Clio and I share notes about progress to this point. Most of the young folk are tired, but everyone made it. Several have blisters from new boots that were broken in, but not broken in while wearing packs. It appears there are no calamities to lessen the sheen of this beautiful valley, and so we parcel out suggestions for establishing camp, which stimulates a frenzy of activity—tents going up, wood gathered and broken for our campfire, water purified. Given the grunts and groans overheard in the background, sleep will be welcomed.

I'm sharing a tent with Clio tonight, a concession to diminish pack weight. Like everyone else, it's lights-out for both of us as soon as darkness settles over camp. Clio rolls to one side muffling a cavernous snore. The last thing I remember is the constant soft music of White River running over cobblestones, around moss-covered granite boulders, and over submerged logs. It's perfect background noise, white noise, and soon I'm deeply, soundly, asleep.

The next thing I know, shafts of subdued yellow are streaming through gaps in the firs—early morning is arriving. Today our trail exits forest for numerous switchbacks up long avalanche paths toward a ridge crest of the Cascade Mountains along Glacier Peak. It's a magical day with sunlight rapidly warming the land. Small, joyous streams are cutting the trail while copses of stunted fir divide broad, green avalanche paths. Wildflowers increase as we gain altitude; they have mostly come and gone down at the warmer, lower elevations.

Glacier Peak begins to appear over the top of a ridge to our north while Indian Head Peak looms large to the south, covered with white snow-fields. When we reach the Pacific Crest Trail it is simply beautiful. Lingering almond-shaped snowbanks cluster in the northern shade of white fir. Small tarns are alive, warmed by summer sun. Marsh marigolds linger at the water's edge. Looking northward, the land undulates with rounded waves of low hillocks and shallow drainages that feed the White River. Jagged peaks fill the southern skyline, sheltering snow from the sun's intensity while Glacier Peak commands the northern view.

We're camping tonight in an eastern lee of the Crest, just enough yards below to avoid the full onslaught of a relentless breeze blowing in from the Pacific Ocean. In spots wildflowers are just peaking. Pasqueflowers reach to midcalf, their bushy heads waving in gentle breezes that sweep the mountainside. Lupine, purple-blue with full blossoms, is interwoven among white, yellow, and orange batons of other flowers in this mosaic, Glacier Peak's flower gardens gone cosmic.

Our unwritten code is no campfires in alpine meadows, and as a practical matter, few trees are around anyway. Most everyone is ready to turn in early, exhausted from the almost 2,000-foot slog from valley floor to ridge crest, in addition to the previous day's marathon mileage. Retreating to our tents, breezes kick up just after sundown and continue blowing just hard enough to flap ripstop nylon with what is, at first, an irritating cadence. Clio seems bothered for about three minutes before he's off to another place, deeply asleep. Soon, the steady beat of wind on tent has become an old friend.

Clio is still snoring lightly at 6:00 A.M., but I hear others rustling outside. These freeze-dried meals lack the punch our group needs after all of this exercise and healthy living—young men are out scavenging. It's time to get up and see about starting the stoves.

By mid-morning we begin to trickle down the trail toward Indian Head Peak and Indian Pass, where we branch off on Indian Creek. As quickly as White River Trail gained elevation toward the Crest and alpine country, Indian Creek Trail loses it. Almost instantly the valley is heavily forested. For a couple of miles we negotiate through thick forest broken by avalanche paths sliding off Indian Head Peak. Eventually these swaths are lost as forest closes in around the trail and only intermittent breaks appear. Our trail is extremely narrow, a good indicator that this valley is seldom visited.

When Clio and I set off ahead of the group to find our next camp, the wilderness becomes suffused with eerie silence. Birdcalls disappear. Sounds of wind stirring the firs are lost in the vacuum of an enormous valley that sees few humans. Only Indian Creek splashes excitedly to our right on the south, breaking quiet laid like a blanket over this valley. Such perfect stillness raises alarm deep within us. Our senses are fully alert, so alert that we do not even have to mention the sensation to each other. Intuitively we know that the forest is on edge, but explanations elude us. What has charged the atmosphere in this immense, lonesome drainage?

Off to the right in a stand of fir lies an appealing campsite with a fire ring, access to a creek, and plenty of downed wood. Another eighth of a mile and forested trail will break out into a broad avalanche path. Clio signals to stop here for a look-see. Over by the fire ring, blatantly in the trail's line of sight, we set packs against trees so that no one will miss the signal—we camp here tonight—and scout around the campsite. How far to access Indian Creek? We can hear its roar and thrashing, but unlike most camps, no easy path is visible because willows eight feet tall and as thick as hair on a shaggy dog screen the waters.

Clio heads uphill a bit and then excitedly calls me over. On the western fringe of our campsite are sparkling fresh remnants of a massive dig. A good-size swimming pool of turf has been methodically plowed within hours, minutes, or perhaps even seconds of our arrival. Clearly the work of a huge bear, soil is turned topsy-turvy with several deeper depressions scattered within the construction project. It appears that someone flew in a rototiller by helicopter and then meticulously went about preparing a large garden for the season.

The havoc speaks for itself. Clio and I just blow hard and look wide-eyed at each other. No wonder Indian Head Peak's forest was so silent. A gargantuan, furry beast was going after something—ground squirrels, tasty roots, or insects—with as much relish as could be mustered. Meanwhile, the rest of the forest, especially vulnerable wildlife, simply vanished or tried to become as inconspicuous as possible—out of sight, out of mind. Clio and I must have made just enough noise to alert the bear of our approach.

Bears in Pacific Northwest wilderness are able to achieve impressive size since vegetation receives abundant precipitation. Grizzly bears tend to stay north of the border, although numerous sightings in remote northern areas of Washington State have been duly registered. It's probably the work of an unusually large black bear, but it has all the characteristics of grizzly foraging. Whether black bear or grizzly, there is no question in our minds that it's gigantic.

Clio and I have a decision to make. We can either tell the teens about the bear, or ignore it. Given the large size of our group there is little sense in trying to track it. With all of the commotion the young ones are making, this bear is probably a good half-mile away by now. Telling them to look out for the bruin will only frighten them and may ruin a budding appreciation for the outdoors. We drop the matter and agree to keep vigilant.

Clio heads south toward Indian Creek, parting dense screens of willows, trying to find our water source. This is lunacy given the obvious evidence of potential bear danger, but he forages onward with faith that is unfailing. Yellow-green willows whip me in the face when I try to keep

This brown colored female black bear has just finished feeding on a carcass. A lucky find as she can use all the protein she can get before winter hibernation.

up with him in charging over cobblestone mounds. A colossal amount of water must move down this valley when snowmelt begins. Finally, ice-blue strands of Indian Creek emerge, rushing east toward the Columbia River. This will do—crystalline water from the Valley of the Mountain Gods; a valley protected by a gigantic sentinel lurking at the forest's edge.

I jerk up and snap to attention. It's almost too quiet. Indian Creek murmurs gently in the distance while an occasional breeze buffets our tent. Other than this, there's a complete vacuum—it's noiseless. In the deep recesses of my mind, hardwiring won't let me slumber. A primal part of me knows that we're encroaching on a large mammal's territory. The sight of a rototilled slope just beyond our camp's reach floods my subconscious and spills into hypersensitive awareness of danger lurking in the fir, among

Younger male subadult grizzly bears tend to get into more conflict with humans as they are forced to use marginal habitat to stay out of ranges claimed by more dominant bears.

the tight copses of willows, or along an avalanche slope two hundred feet away.

"Go to sleep!"

I shout back to needling little hobgoblins who patter on about an imminent attack. Unfortunately I know that rip-stop nylon won't stop razor-sharp claws from entering and snatching a tasty morsel. Whose tent will be most allur-ing because it's the smallest and farthest away from the safety of the masses? Which camper disregarded our ad-monitions to hang all food tonight? What are the prospects that a grizzly bear has wandered down from Canada to this pristinely remote, seldom-visited canyon? And, if it wasn't a grizzly that left the excavation, is this the mother of all black bears?

TO TENT OR NOT TO TENT?
THAT IS THE QUESTION

You have just reached a campsite five miles from the trailhead. The wilderness you are visiting harbors a healthy population of black bears and a few unsubstan-tiated grizzly bear sightings have been recorded. Is it better to sleep in a tent, or not?

In answering this question it is first essential to rec-ognize that no evidence is available to suggest that black bears differ from grizzly bears when it comes to this decision. A tent serves as a critical psychological obstacle to *virtually any* bear because it is man-made. Therefore, sleeping in a tent (as opposed to sleeping out in the open) lowers the probability of being attacked by a bear at night. However, the matter isn't that simple.

Size of a tent is critical. Bears may nip the side of a tent to investigate what's inside. If a person is crammed into a tent and touching the tent wall, this could reinforce a bear's initial suspicion that a food source is within. Tents that tower over bears may be more intimidating to them.

On the other hand, the safety of a tent becomes a liability if a bear does prey on those inside. A collapsed tent swaddles occupants in a binding grip of ripstop nylon, canvas, or other relatively strong material. This immobilizes the occupants and turns the advantage in favor of the predator. It could become difficult to extricate yourself, to use bear spray, or to discharge a firearm under these circumstances.

Bear expert Stephen Herrero, in *Bear Attacks: Their Causes and Avoidance*, notes: "My data strongly suggest that people sleeping without tents were more likely to be injured, even killed, than were people who slept in tents."

Use a tent. Keep a pocketknife handy to cut your way out, and a can of pepper spray ready for defensive purposes.

At 1:00 A.M. I'm sound asleep, mentally worn out from anxiety, when a branch snaps fifty feet away by the trail. Immediately, my heart begins thumping like a bass drum playing a fiery beat, and my eyes open saucer-wide as I search for even a smidgen of light. Pure adrenaline surges through my veins as I grope for a flashlight and Swiss Army knife in case

A mature female grizzly during a fall snowstorm. Bears will often stay near their denning areas and wait for adequate snow to cover their tracks before heading into the winter den.

I have to cut my way out of the tent. My hearing ratchets up two levels, detecting faint footfalls. It's not a camper heading to the bushes; this is an animal skirting our campsite out there.

Waiting . . .

I hold my breath so that it's easier to read the direction and size of the intruder. Another few thumps finally tail off into nothingness. Were those heavy pads of a bear or hooves of an elk making those thumps? Should I go outside and spark a confrontation, or leave well enough alone? Reasoning tells me to stay put; why bargain for trouble when there is none? But, primeval fear screams to gather the troops. In the end I settle on remaining vigilant. If the noise ramps up in any way, shape, or form, I'll take action.

Absolute quiet settles over our camp—an eerie silence that is almost too hushed, and for all intents and purposes, artificial. Perhaps I'm not the only one that snapped to attention. I bet some of the young folk are also awake and scared out of their wits. Are we unknowingly sending intuitive primordial messages, warning this perpetrator to stay away? Can a grizzly or black bear read our minds? Will these collective thoughts repel such a guest? I wait. And, wait. Whatever was out there moves off, leaving us alone and hunkering in down-filled sleeping bags.

A robin begins singing loudly, forcefully, directly above our tent. Clio turns over again. It's barely 5:00 A.M. but I'm wide awake now. Rustling outside tells me that the young men are once again desperate for breakfast. This time I can teach them most by not leaving my sleeping bag. They know what to do and how to do it, maybe not efficiently, but perhaps with a little trial and error. I can best pass on my knowledge by not intervening. Clio and I lay waiting in our nest while the young folk rise to the occasion, creating a communal meal.

Not surprisingly, everyone is eager to get going. They want to be home with their friends and comforts. How their faces shine with happiness and beatific smiles. Somehow that sheen was not there when we began this trip.

They want to get home as quickly as possible; so do Clio and I. But we hope that their lives have been touched just enough by this backcountry adventure. If we have done our job, we've passed on memories of pure snowmelt flowing over round river cobblestones, breezes singing through towering spires of fir and cedar, tapestries of vivid flowers dancing in sunlight, bears that go bump in the night, and vistas too beautiful for words. Hopefully in the course of their lives these young folk will improve the earth rather than only take from it. Perhaps they too will pass on this gift to others.

9 ❧

THE MAGIC OF WILDNESS

I never dreamed that a person might actually run into a snarling hump of stinky fur so close to civilization. But after reading about a rash of bear encounters along the western front of the San Gabriel Mountains that bracket Los Angeles's northern fringes, I realized this was indeed a reality. What a fascinating prospect! Within sight of millions of people, bears—wild backcountry beasts—are roaming free as could be on the very trails I intend to hike. This stupefying revelation is both exciting and slightly terrifying. Such a possibility also sends a chilling alarm racing through my mind: What happens if I actually run into one of these brutes? What then?

A lingering obsession with bears begins the moment I realize they might actually be

A yearling black bear cub in the safety of a large tree.

walking the exact same paths I will be walking. With a neophyte's naiveté, I assumed that bear encounters only happened to unlucky people in other places, especially in true scenic wilderness like Alaska or the Sierras—not the hills of Los Angeles. Apprehension added a slightly acidic taste to the prospect of coming face-to-face with an animal capable of serious mischief. Even if you read all of the literature, it still doesn't prepare you for that initial shocking moment when a startled, drooling bear is a scant twenty yards away, woofing, and you're all alone.

Despite all of the warnings, I am determined to enjoy a bit of back-country exploration. How will I react if a big, black mass of muscle, fat, and fur comes waddling toward me? Only time will tell . . .

All day long clouds and sun have been waging a wonderfully theatric battle over Los Angeles. No sooner is the sun blocked with temperatures plummeting before whirlwinds swirl away the cover and radiant life returns with penetrating warmth. Driving to Pasadena and a trail running up Arroyo Seco Canyon behind Jet Propulsion Laboratory, there are no intentions of getting very far into wilderness. I simply want some solitude; a reprieve from raucous car exhausts, slamming doors, loud radios in the neighborhood, barking dogs defending apartment balconies, and boisterous arguments among loving partners.

Midafternoon traffic is fairly heavy as throngs of cars clog the Ventura Freeway—what a way to live. By the time Pasadena's exit creeps up, I'm ready to dump Los Angeles. Too many people, too many cars; life has to be better than this. A trail guide suggests parking by the laboratory, but the easily accessible lot conjures anxious thoughts. Is parking permissible for the public? Are cars parking here targets for thieves? Is the lot being watched this very minute by desperados?

Welcome to Los Angeles.

Following the trail guide's detailed instructions, I'm headed north from the lot. Passing a laboratory guard, I expect to be interrogated at length about my intentions. However, he pays absolutely no interest as I skirt a fence and enter the junglelike growth of willows, bamboo, and chaparral shrubs. The laboratory fortress looms to the west; hovering over the trail and raising skepticism about whether this effort is worth it—

worth the hassle of getting here. Paralleling the fence, a trail hunts through thick vegetation screening hush-hush, foreboding ambitions at the Lab. A trickle of water is audible and the rich smell of wet earth, damp growth, and life overwhelm my senses.

Soon the trail is alongside what amounts to a very decent little stream, fresh with scurrying water pushing bits of gravel along a serpentine valley floor. Steep canyon walls laced with boulders rise rapidly above the enchanting streambed, embracing it protectively from urban shock just yards away. Hillsides are covered in low-lying brush; dense, gray-brown, and dry, it's perfect fodder for wildfire. From down in the canyon it's difficult to see what the cliffs rise toward, but the ravine deepens and Arroyo Seco's trail dives for the streambed with its steady flow.

On reaching streamside a thrilling thought floods my mind. Here I am no more than a quarter-mile beyond the Jet Propulsion Laboratory compound, and yet I have crossed a definable threshold into wilderness. You cannot see, hear, or smell the Lab, but it's back there, a few hundred yards, make no mistake about that. Wildness and solitude fill Arroyo Seco Canyon. It harbors almost nothing in the way of visible human touch, and civilization will be left far behind on leaping across the flowing waters.

Perfect bear country ahead . . .

Arroyo Seco's stream is obviously swollen with runoff from previous storms. It seems to possess a slightly wild character coursing down the canyon, which is laden with bits of decomposed granite. In dry times the stream is undoubtedly more tranquil, perhaps only flowing beneath a sandy surface. My trail curves around a rocky corner to the left, but given impenetrable brush, it's impossible to see what lies ahead. If the San Gabriels are rife with bears, how about this remote and seldom-used arroyo? To find out, all I have to do is jump over the stream and keep going for several miles. It's as simple as that.

BEARS IN THE SAN GABRIEL MOUNTAINS

The famous naturalist and field biologist Joseph Grinnell studied the presence of bears throughout Southern California. As a tribute to his scientific accomplishments,

Grinnell's name graces one of Glacier National Park's famous glaciers—the Grinnell Glacier. In a 1938 *Sierra Club Bulletin*, Dr. Grinnell published a treatise about bears in California distilled from a book he previously coauthored (Grinnell, Dixon, and Linsdale, *Fur-Bearing Mammals of California*, University of California Press, 1937).

Grinnell made an important distinction between black bears and grizzly bears, suggesting that grizzly bears represented the ultimate embodiment of what Californians conceived a bear to be. In early California black bears roamed forest and mountain habitats while grizzly bears foraged throughout lowlands and foothills. Thus, people had more grizzly encounters than run-ins with black bears. This pattern changed in a big way as civilization gradually encroached on the lowlands. Grizzly bears were progressively driven into mountain wilderness areas, eventually displacing black bears.

The San Gabriel Mountains offer a perfect example of grizzly migration. Ringing the northeastern sides of the Los Angeles basin, these almost impenetrable mountains provided exceptional black bear habitat. However, as the urban population grew, grizzlies were inadvertently pushed further into the hills. Their superior size made them more than a match for black bears, who retreated deeper into mountainous reaches as well as migrating to southern ranges.

As a boy, Grinnell lived in Pasadena during the late 1880s. He recounts following grizzly bear tracks in the vicinity of the West Fork of the San Gabriel River. Admitting to a burning lust for a grizzly kill, Grinnell chased bear sign with rifle in hand until the trail entered chaparral. Then he followed right after the bruin, pushing his gun out in front as he crawled along on hands and knees. Grinnell was determined to replicate the heroism of another Pasadena lad who shot a grizzly in the San Gabriels and gained a bit of notoriety.

In 1916 the last grizzly in the San Gabriels was killed after it raided a local vineyard. Throughout California the great bear which graces the Golden State's flag had methodically been exterminated. In part their demise can be explained by their lack of adaptability compared to black bears. Grinnell observed that California's lowland grizzles apparently did not hibernate like black bears high up in the forests. This made grizzles more susceptible to year-round run-ins with people and eventually contributed to their extirpation.

Preparing to take the leap, a gnawing intuitive feeling takes over that something far more magnificent waits up canyon. With limited time to explore this day, it'll be impossible to fully capture this unknown and waiting gift, but instinctively I know it's there—the thrill of uncharted territory. Until there's more time to explore I'm fully content with the merry stream flowing raucously at my side and the birds calling and flitting about in dense green brush. The scents of life are heady, reeking of fecund earth and the unimaginable possibilities of nature gone wild; the visual peace of a canyon driven by the perfect interplay of rock, greenery, and upslope; and, the sound of wilderness bereft of the city's hum while mere yards distant.

I leap over the stream, part the veil of wildness, and begin the quest. Bears, magnificent tranquil pools, showy wildflowers, secret forested glens—does anyone truly know what waits ahead? That's the magic of wilderness—you never know what to expect down these backcountry paths.

Mostly it's the unpredicted that materializes, but its flavor is seldom disappointing, just different, and in many cases, superior. Seek bears; find waterfall. Search for wildflowers; discover a colossal river of boulders. Hunt for an inspirational viewpoint; sight a red-tailed hawk gliding effortlessly on the wind. Bears are always dear to my heart, but they're also found in wild-lands that are breathtakingly amazing. Come to think of it, perhaps bears are simply an excuse to find this magic and wallow deeply in its embrace.

Looking for bears? What finer place to search than the Grand Tetons? This ecosystem provides a rich wilderness setting where we're the visitors and bears are permanent residents. Part of the fun in visiting the Grand Tetons is the prospect of encountering charismatic megafauna—moose, buffalo, elk, and grizzly or black bear—when you least expect it. For many people this possibility is terrifying, and causes them to stay away entirely, or at least remain confined to the safety of developed areas. For others the presence of mammals capable of inflicting serious physical damage places a razor edge on any park visit. And, after having been there and survived, you look back on such experiences not with regret, but with unbounded enthusiasm.

In Scott McMillion's book, *Mark of the Grizzly*, Tom Murphy, a wildlife photographer from Livingston, Montana, located on the edge of the Teton-Yellowstone ecosystem, vividly conveys how charismatic mam-mals enhance outdoor adventure:

> *Just being in grizzly country can be incredibly exhilarating, even if the bears are at a distance. You don't need to get close to get the feeling. The thing that I really like about traveling or hiking in country where you know there are grizzly bears is that your hearing improves, your eyesight improves, your sense of smell improves. You're paying attention a lot more. You're a lot more alive if you're paying attention to bears.*

Even for those who see only fear, the fact is that their outdoor experience will be heightened. It isn't like a typical day's drive down to the local Wal-Mart or a brief stop at Starbucks. A visit to the Grand Tetons, or any wilder-ness, injects much-needed excitement into our everyday civilized lives.

Late spring is an excellent time to mount an expedition for sighting bears. They've left hibernation and migrate to valley basins where fresh growth

Blooming clover is a favorite food of bears. This alert grizzly might spend days in this field of clover eating almost nonstop.

awaits, as well as a bounty of newborn elk and moose calves. It's an in-between season when winter doesn't dominate and broiling summer is too far in the future to contemplate. Best of all, this is a time when campgrounds and trails are virtually empty. The potential for adventure close to the edge of the back-country multiplies. You are more likely to see, hear, smell, taste, and feel un-trammeled wildness. Great temperature swings and precipitation can be anticipated, but that's all part of the adventure. Encounters with wildlife are highly probable. In short, the in-between season is one of the best-kept secrets when it comes to successfully spotting elusive bruins.

Elk, buffalo, and antelope seem to be everywhere as day fades to night, especially down in little, hidden hollows, on benches above the Snake River, and along forested edges of meadows, because the upper reaches of the Tetons and Yellowstone are packed with snow. Elk are particularly numerous on sage-filled benches overlooking the vibrant Snake River. Small herds of shaggy bison lumber along the road like decrepit dump trucks having it en-tirely their way, and bound for pitch-black glens with succulent grass.

Darkness finally arrives and with it the prospect of rest after a long day of traveling to Grand Teton National Park. I'm huddled in a little cabin on Colter Bay that serves as base camp. Biting cold air is seeping through ancient log walls that have seen better days. It might be full-bore summer south of the Wyoming state line, but up here in late May, it's still very early spring. Latent crusty snowdrifts collaring fir trees around the cabin prove that warm weather is merely a theory. It almost hurts to breathe the pure, chilly air, but it just doesn't matter—there's adventure waiting outside these log walls, and bears to find in the majestic Tetons.

Next morning the initial reconnoiter commences, and I'm following a heavily used trail along crystal-clear Jackson Lake. I've spent fifteen minutes glassing far-off avalanche slopes radiant with sun, hoping to spy any bears—black or grizzly—out grazing on early seasonal greens. Admittedly, grizzly bears are generally found in more northerly areas of the Tetons, particularly northeast toward Yellowstone. But that's part of the magic in

looking for them: much depends on luck and tenacity. If you're not out there at dawn or dusk, your chances for a sighting diminish. If you don't have your binoculars up and scanning, your odds shrink for seeing something.

A large part of successful wildlife viewing essentially boils down to hard work plus luck. Although the probability for sightings can be raised simply by following various rules of thumb, special moments tend to unfold in spite of your best preparations. One trail is selected over another and nothing unusual happens. The next time out it may be completely the opposite. In

The real key to wildlife viewing is just being in the right place at the right time. Generally early morning and late afternoons are the best times. Next have good binoculars or spotting scope. View wildlife from a distance so as not to disturb.

fact, I've found that the best way *not* to see what I'm looking for is to intentionally go looking for it. I'm far more successful when I focus on a promising location where wildlife sightings frequently occur rather than targeting a specific species. Great habitat almost always delivers action-packed entertainment.

At the moment I'm looking for movement; any little change on the hillsides that might signal a large mammal. Once movement is detected, then I can drill down to identify exactly what's sauntering along. Distance implies superior optics, necessary in order to hone in on suspected animals, and nothing beats a fine pair of binoculars. Being too far away is unacceptable to some—they have to be right on top of a moose, elk, wolf, bison, bear, or other critter to feel that they had an actual encounter. Not I; if an animal can be seen clearly through binoculars, I'm satisfied. Distance does not devalue the experience. In truth, I actually feel better about distant viewings because it impacts wildlife to a lesser degree.

After fifteen minutes of seeing nothing I move along, since morning has just dawned. Perhaps this afternoon or evening, or maybe tomorrow morning, the hillside will be graced by a bear. It's just a matter of time and effort to keep looking even though nothing has turned up dozens of times before. Dropping the binoculars gives me a chance to focus on this captivating path that winds over and around tree roots, darting out to the lakeshore and running back to forest.

Eventually my trail turns east toward several little lakes and ponds—perfect habitat for hawks, eagles, osprey, swans, ducks, geese, muskrats, and even moose. I cinch the hood of my parka down a little tighter. Here, the early-morning temperature is dropping to its lowest ebb, until it rises with the tree-obscured sun. It's just damn cold despite my gloves, hat, and high-tech clothing. I keep walking at a brisk pace to build up some heat, lost in thought about where to hike later this afternoon. Then, without warning, magic unfolds.

An osprey swoops overhead with a fish dangling from its talons. It's on final approach to a nest high in a long-dead lodgepole pine situated with a perfect view over Jackson Lake. Fledglings' screeching cries give them away. Their two-foot-high nest is a tangled mass of thick sticks that

The fun with wildlife viewing is you never really know what the day will bring. Some days are just lucky!

resembles Poseidon's hairdo. Perfectly placed with an osprey-eye vantage over this fish-rich lake, the young ones are secure along the rocky, relatively inaccessible lakeshore, hidden from most predators. After a clumsy landing, parent osprey—most likely a male since they tend to deliver food to nesting females and chicks—methodically tears the fish into shreds before filling demanding mouths. Minutes later mealtime is over, and the parent flies off to repeat the cycle.

From here the path leaves Jackson Lake and enters scraggly lodgepole pine forest, past intermittent meadows filled with dark-green sage, now covered in crystal-white frost. I can feel my concentration kick up several levels in anticipation of wild animals. This is a perfect time for running into big mammals as the osprey encounter amply suggests. Going into stealth mode, I'm a little more careful about brushing the arms of my coat against my body; determined to keep my breathing as quiet as can be.

Approaching Swan Lake a half-mile later, walking as silently as possible on packed, dank soil, scattered gravel, and resinous pine needles, I creep toward its shore. Frosty sun is just beginning to shine through the distant trees, and I maneuver among spindly pines on the western shore, seeking warmth.

At lake's edge, less than thirty yards away, is a moose feeding serenely in dark blue waters. One hundred yards beyond is a monstrous bull moose sporting an unbelievable rack; he's wading in deep water, searching out luxuriant bottom growth. Trumpeter swans ply the lake at its eastern end. In a truly golden moment, sun bursts radiantly onto the lake, heralding a new day. Then it dawns on me that the nearest moose seems to be heading my way.

No worries.

The moose is not the least bit interested in me—or so I think, until it closes the gap by fifteen yards, twelve yards . . . still coming purposefully in my direction. I decide to get behind a large pine, two feet in diameter, as the moose saunters up from shore. It continues to waddle steadily toward me, now only ten yards away. Suddenly, I wake up; the moose's intentions become totally transparent. If I don't do something quickly in the next few seconds, I'm going to have a good-size moose right on top of me!

Two choices present themselves: One is to maintain my position behind this large lodgepole pine to create a barrier between us (I've watched a similar tactic employed by several people cornered by a humongous

Moose can be very unpredictable, especially after the bulls have cleaned their antlers.

bull elk in Banff National Park). The second, and better, choice derives from something I have read somewhere, sometime, about deer. Ungulates do not like to enter forested areas with blowdowns or widely fallen trees, ostensibly due to an intuitive fear of breaking their legs.

Twenty feet to my left is a mound of fallen pine trees, each one about eight to twelve inches in diameter, all randomly piled together to a height of about five feet. Running to the logs, I beat the now-charging moose with about a second to spare. I clamber up the pile of overgrown match-sticks to a height equivalent with the moose's shoulder. Now the test comes. The moose is definitely showing aggression, but it appears that I've gotten the upper hand. It stands panting heavily, glaring at me—stale-mate. After several minutes it wanders off to wade back into Swan Lake. Able to breathe again and trying to relax despite a massive infusion of adrenaline in my system, I casually hop off the pile and finish my amble around the lake. I wanted adventure; I certainly found it.

It's been a tremendously eventful morning despite my obsessive-compulsive desire to view, even from long distance, a grizzly bear. The amazing fact is that so much life can be packed into Jackson Hole. There's so much to see that I've almost forgotten why I came here in the first place. It seems like every time I turn another corner, a new discovery awaits. If not a bison, an eagle. If not a pair of trumpeter swans, an elk. If not a captivating curve in the Snake River, a moose browsing on fresh wil-low shoots. Does anyone actually need to see a bear when wildlife is liter-ally spilling over throughout the park?

Later that afternoon I decide to return to Swan Lake using an eastern, more forested route. Where there's moose, there may be bear—some-times all it takes is to think positive thoughts and your wish is fulfilled. This more easterly path drops steeply down a rough hill with patches of lodgepole pines spread about like spots on a Dalmatian, eventually inter-secting the main trail I used earlier this morning. By now the temperature has climbed past warm, almost hot, so shade feels good. In fact, heat's warm embrace is so comfortable that after a big lunch I'm a bit sleepy, and not paying close attention to the surrounding forest. When you're in the Tetons you should know better.

Out of the corner of my eye I catch a tiny movement and instantly freeze. Twenty-five feet away at the edge of this lodgepole pine forest, with copses of aspen strewn about, is a cow moose with calf. From my early-morning encounter it's easy to figure out how dangerous this predicament is. Unfortunately, there's no convenient pile of downed trees offering an easy means for escape. There doesn't appear to be any other option but to apply the same rule of thumb used for an encounter with a grizzly bear and cub. Running could entice the cow to come

Cow moose with calves are extremely protective mothers. Even bears approach with caution, yet grizzlies in Alaska take a number of young calves in the spring and early summer.

after me. Continuing to stare at the moose only suggests aggression. I immediately avert my sight down and to the side—acknowledging her dominance. Then I begin slowly backing up, directly away from her in an off-trail detour. Like a lucky contestant on *The Price is Right*, I choose the correct door, and it pays off—the moose remain hidden in the forest watching; waiting.

As many forest rangers admonish, marauding moose are far more dangerous than people tend to think. In fact, human complacency probably makes moose encounters at least equivalent with bear encounters on the jeopardy scale. For those who only envision cuddly Bullwinkle caricatures whenever they see moose in magazine photographs or on television, there's an entirely different dimension of moose to learn about and respect. For me the classic image is one that unfolded in Denali National Park, when a female moose aggressively pursued a grizzly bear that had been preying on her young—a ton-plus on hooves is enough to dissuade any smart bear. Moose help to keep all of us honest.

REELING WITH LAUGHTER WHILE RAFTING SNAKE RIVER

One of Grand Teton Park's main attractions is the sensuously winding Snake River. What better way to blend into the scenery to an extent that most animals hardly register your presence? Rafting raises the likelihood of seeing wildlife—perhaps an ideal recipe for scaring up some bears? A spring rafting trip is also a perfect means for slowing down the pace of living and getting away from ever-present automobiles. Furthermore, rafting is just what the doctor ordered for those who've lost their zest for life. It's hard to climb aboard a raft and not immediately revert back to the fun times of youth.

Numerous rafting outfitters serve Grand Teton National Park with a variety of floats to pique almost everyone's interest. I'm not looking for Class III and IV thrills, just a mellow float to scope out wild beasts. After rooting through various brochures at the park's visitor center, a promising outfit surfaces and agrees to meet me at Deadman's Bar Landing the next morning. By the time I find put-in, several small groups are milling around the parking lot, chatting with our guides. Two hundred feet away, two rafts are waiting along the river's edge—bulbous blue vessels that look like they've been on a high-fat diet for too long.

Out of courtesy, I defer to a middle-aged couple. They're walking ahead of me as we make our way down to the rafts. Striding along, the woman is parceling out all sorts of abuse to her partner for what she calls, "this stupid idea of yours." Having learned long ago to keep my mouth shut at moments like this, I can't help feeling sorry for the poor fellow. Undoubtedly he also saw the Snake River gleaming like a serpentine viper and was inexorably drawn to a little escapade; perhaps a chance to jump back thirty years to a time when he used to roam the woods, free of this pathetic nagging.

Almost immediately cosmic justice prevails when we drop down a two-foot wet, slippery, and muddy bank to cobblestone-infested river bottom. Unfortunately for the woman, she decided to wear the most luminously white slacks on the face of this earth. It was a fitting choice for shopping in trendy little boutiques in downtown Jackson, but a very inadvisable one for rafting. However, the real problem was not the pants, but the blindingly white tennis shoes with apparently no tread whatsoever. At the two-foot incline she takes a most impressive butt flop—her feet slip right out from under her.

Fellow rafters have probably never heard a woman of her maturity and bearing utter such trashy language. With a grin I turn to the fellow behind me who snickers and then rates the butt flop a "9." I whisper back that it really deserves a "10" for technical superiority, lack of grace, and creativity of verbalization. Whatever the score, it is one of those totally unexpected, but completely unforgettable, moments that happens serendipitously in the wild.

Alas, the magic is not entirely over as our guide shoves us out into the Snake's persistently swift flow. The Snake River is very gentle even in spring. We do not seek, nor experience, any sort of white-water danger. The trip is not billed as such—only a float down the Snake. But, within five minutes of launch, it's as though we're in the middle of wilderness. What a fantastic metamorphosis! It's easy to forget that the main Jackson Hole–Yellowstone road parallels this river at a modest distance. Numerous pull-outs along this road offer convenient opportunities for gazing down on this symbolically vital river. However, once you get on the water it's as though you were transported to the middle of Idaho, Alaska, or any other locale blessed with a Wild and Scenic River.

We float along, discussing the high water level and murkiness due to runoff. Our guide describes vegetation types—which all look like willow to me—and how they support the moose population. As we round a bend, we see several deer drinking at the water's edge, but moose and bears elude us the entire trip. Sometimes magic happens and sometimes it doesn't. In this case a midday trip is working against any bear sightings; they're probably bedded down for the day in timber far away from the Snake River.

Bright sun sparkles off the Snake's smallest waves, and a tender, cool breeze caresses our group in concert with the river's flow. Except for occasional trumpeting of cow moose hidden in the willows, it's calm and peaceful. Actually, the real trumpeting comes from our lady in white on the front of the raft, squawking at this trifle or that. The rest of us are enjoying the sublime beauty of the Tetons. Who cares about her tantrums? We glide down the Snake entranced by the river and the towering, jagged mountains to the west; dominant and snow-covered—imposing mountains of the best sort. Other than the poor, miserable woman, we reap a legendary return on our investment—a return that even Wall Street did not provide with the best technology stocks at the height of the dot-com phenomenon.

Although a spring visit to the Tetons delivered the sort of exciting out-door experiences that everyone deserves to enjoy, it didn't deliver even one puny black bear sighting, much less a subadult grizzly. However, the danger of moose attack was exhilarating; the raft ride was heady. Wilder-ness literally envelops visitors in the Grand Tetons, and without a doubt, I will return at the next opportunity.

The day after Labor Day has all of the characteristics of perfect timing for the Grand Tetons. School is back in session. Families have finished their vacations so national parks exhale a bit as tourism drops. Weather is cooling off and bears enter hyperphagia in preparation for hibernation. They're scarfing up all the calories they can find, which means the poten-tial for more sightings because they are constantly roaming around, look-ing for food. If spring in the Tetons doesn't deliver bears, perhaps fall will.

Today my friend Dick and I have targeted Cascade Canyon as our trail of choice. Two other hiking buddies backpacked up this canyon last year. They reported running into a gigantic black bear prowling the upper reaches of the valley, which made for a fright-filled but stimulating night. Our mission is to find this bear or one of its family members. With the crowds of summer gone, chances favor a sighting if we just play our cards right. At least, that's the assumption made when planning this trip.

Hiking around Jenny Lake to the boat dock and trailhead up Cascade Canyon, an amazing fact becomes all too apparent: People are literally everywhere. After a few minutes of hiking up Cascade Canyon Trail, it's obvious that people are crawling all over the place. A flotilla of ships seems to have ferried almost every park visitor across the lake to join us. Most of them are hiking in slow motion, picking their way up switchbacks among enormous granite boulders. What a zoo. New York City's streets at rush hour are vacant by comparison. Dick and I press on ahead to an over-look of Jenny Lake and stop for lunch. Within ten minutes the hordes ar-rive and decide to sit right next to us. Somehow this isn't what we had in mind as a wilderness outing.

Hastily finishing lunch so that we can move on, Dick asks me, "Have you noticed something unusual about the people?"

"Yeah—there's lot's of them," I reply.

"No, that's not it."

"They're all slow?"

"No. Their average age must be midseventies-plus."

I can't ever remember seeing so many seniors out on the trail at one time. But, it's good that they're outside doing it. Like us, they scheduled the Tetons after summer's hordes departed. Like us, they thought they would find the park empty. Like us, they chose the park's most beautiful canyon trail because they thought that nobody would be up here. Like us, they're not going to turn back for anyone or anything.

Continuing up Cascade Canyon, the scenery is absolutely stunning, with translucent water sliding gracefully over rounded granite slabs, then pooling before beginning another cascade. The streambed is perfectly visible; pure mountain water flowing over gray-white granite blocks reflects the sparkling sun. Obviously Cascade Canyon's name doesn't come from the falls entering Jenny Lake, but rather, from the water that gradually cascades over low rockfalls throughout the canyon.

We wander among huge boulders along gentle cascades toward the canyon's western terminus. Dick wants to press on, reluctant to quit. Long ago we gave up any hope of sighting a bear because this poor canyon is just inundated by too many people. His insistence makes all the difference in the world. Around the next bend another faultless scene unfolds with canyon walls broadening—the portrait of a perfect glacial valley. On each side the most beautiful granite rock with castlelike spires reaches vertically toward the heavens. Lodgepole pine and spruce blanket the valley floor. It's so stunning that it seems surreal.

Rounding this last bend we run into an energized foursome. They excitedly inform us about a mammoth bull moose grazing on willow shrubs around the corner. Twenty yards off trail is a magnificently humongous beast. Dick grabs his camera and goes in for a close-up, saying, "Hold my pack. If he charges, spray some of that bear spray to save me."

How it happens that Dick walks so near to that big bull and takes pictures for about fifteen minutes is beyond comprehension. The bull simply ignores him even though Dick is essentially in his face. Vestiges of a felt-like substance hang from several of the rack's tines. What a splendid animal. He's in his prime, with a thick, lustrous coat all ready for winter and the Teton's legendary bitter cold. Eventually he'll drop out of this canyon to winter around the valley floor. Up here in Cascade Canyon, he knows few predators. Grizzly bears supposedly only range down to Moran Canyon, two valleys north of Cascade Canyon. Wolves are roaming the northern end of Grand Teton National Park. In time these predators too will migrate to this lovely canyon.

Dick finishes taking photos and crawls out of the brush, causing absolutely no reaction from the bull. The outcome would probably have been quite different if it had been me pulling the same stunt. Back on the trail we gaze one last time up Cascade Canyon. It seems to go on for miles. The highest ramparts remain snow free as the warming sun melts the latest dusting from a few days before. It's been a truly remarkable visit to Cascade Canyon. West, seemingly within a stone's throw, the terminus of this trail splits, one route heading north and the other, south. Our friends who camped in these upper reaches saw black bear and elk, a dream that doesn't materialize for us.

Having accepted that we wouldn't see any wildlife due to so many people, today's journey took an unexpected turn. We didn't see bear, but we came up close and personal with a huge bull moose. That's the enchantment of the wilderness. You never know what to expect. A supremely large bull moose is more than adequate compensation for not sighting a bear. In fact, deep in the recesses of our minds as we trundle along the trail, Dick and I feel lucky that we escaped with our lives in view of previous moose encounters.

Down on the flat shoreline we turn north toward the parking lot. The way back is exactly what we expected—empty trail through awe-inspiring country. The day cools slightly while the sun softens. We're walking through the shade of a healthy pine and spruce forest. Life is good; too good. How did we ever deserve this? The fact that we didn't see any bear diminishes to what it is—irrelevant against the granite backdrop of Teton spires, a merry cascading stream, a honking huge bull moose, and brilliant jade-green water along Jenny Lake's shore.

❖

They say the third time's a charm, so another bear-viewing trip to Grand Teton National Park is scheduled. Like previous trips to the Tetons, Colter Bay is base camp. It's rustic, inexpensive, centrally located, and down-to-earth. However, this time I'm going to purposefully avoid patterns and places I've followed in the past. These rituals certainly haven't paid off in bear sightings. It's time to inject a good measure of contrarian thinking in these expeditions.

Rather than spectacular country, I'll search out the more mundane. Instead of walking high-profile trails, I'll look for backwater paths that are overlooked as summer season matures. As a substitute for bona fide bear habitat, I'll look in places that even clever coyotes would shun while summer reaches its apex. As opposed to exploring the lush central and northern parts of the park, I'll head south toward the park boundary where people are more likely to impinge year-round. Instead of those frigid early-morning forays, I'll get a late start.

Grizzly bears are smart! They will return to areas where they have had success hunting in the past. This may mean going to certain traditional areas where elk, bison, moose, or deer give birth.

Taggart Lake, sitting at 6,902 feet within a stone's throw of Moose Junction, is my initial destination, with a side trip to Bradley Lake, a mile away and 120 feet higher. Why this spot? So many valleys flowing east off the Teton crest have overused trails penetrating to alpine lakes, spectacular overlooks, raging waterfalls, or rock-climbing access points. Taggart Lake is fed by namesake Taggart Creek, spawned out of Avalanche Canyon. Most importantly, there is no formal trail up this canyon.

The Teton crest and peaks above Taggart Lake are arguably less impressive than spires immediately north—Middle Teton, Mount Owen, and Teewinot—peaks with high cachet. Given Taggart Lake's southern location, it's improbable that grizzly bears have roamed this far; there's just too much human encroachment and not enough forage. Adding all of these factors together, what better trail to pick as a contrarian option? Furthermore, I'm going with an attitude—a chip on my shoulder. I really don't care anymore if I ever see a bear in the Tetons. Instead, bring on the moose for which Taggart and Bradley Lakes are renowned. Dense willow thickets, perfect moose habitat, grew after a fire devoured forest that formerly cascaded down to Teton Park Road.

BEAR SIGHTINGS INCREASE IN GRAND TETON NATIONAL PARK?

Are bear sightings increasing in Grand Teton National Park? Fairly accurate information is available about grizzly bear encounters in the park, but less so for black bears, which do not have a reputation for fatal encounters. Although caution should be used regarding the reliability of product testimonials, UDAP Industries (www.udap.com) provides a very interesting source of information (on their Web-page testimonials) about black bear encounters in Grand Teton National Park.

UDAP was founded by Mark Matheny after he suffered a severe mauling by a grizzly bear while bow hunting. Matheny and his partner, Dr. Fred Bahnson, were hunting mule deer northwest of Yellowstone National Park in September 1992 when they surprised a sow with two cubs. The sow pounced on Matheny as he ran up trail. Bahnson, who courageously came to rescue his friend, was carrying a can of self-defense pepper spray intended for urban settings. The spray worked, and both hunters escaped with their lives. Matheny was so impressed with the spray's results—even though it was designed to shoot a narrow spray pattern targeted at humans—that he devised a new product known as PepperPower to deter grizzly bears.

Among the UDAP testimonials, Garry Lineback describes his run-in with a 300-pound black bear sow with two cubs near Bradley and Taggart Lakes in Grand Teton National Park. Lineback began backing away from the sow, but she continued to pursue him until he unleashed a blast of PepperPower. That was enough to stop her predacious behavior and send her packing. Brett Jackson also testifies about UDAP's lifesaving prowess. Jackson was hiking with his father and brother at Jenny Lake when they surprised a black bear feeding alongside a very heavily used trail. The bear charged twice before the trio blasted it with PepperPower, after which it retreated to higher ground, trying to wipe off the spray.

Grizzly bear encounters in Grand Teton National Park and bordering areas capture more attention and seem to be increasing in frequency. It is possible this is simply a reflection of more reports being made public. Nonetheless, grizzlies have been slowly migrating south in the Greater Yellowstone Ecosystem. Dave Moody, trophy game coordinator for the Wyoming Game and Fish Department, acknowledges documented grizzly bear activity as far down as Jenny Lake.

Recently, an angler fishing the Snake River near Flagg Ranch, along the main highway leading to Yellowstone National Park, tussled with an aggressive grizzly. The bear attacked Ken Bates's left arm before Ken was able to punch the bear in the eye. The grizzly backed off and eventually fled when a motorist came to the rescue.

Moran Junction is well south of Flagg Ranch in the eastern part of the park. In 2001, an elk hunter, Conrad Smith of Minnesota, surprised a sow with cub. Conrad could not reach the pepper spray he was carrying so he played dead. The sow mauled him before running away leaving him battered and bruised, but alive.

These and other run-ins suggest a rising number of bear encounters—both black bear and grizzly—within the confines and outlying areas of Grand Teton National Park. Although people usually think of Yellowstone as the center of bear conflicts, the Tetons appear to be gaining a similar reputation.

Taggart Creek parking lot is pretty expansive. This is a popular destination in winter, and even more so as spring unfolds. Add the lakes and you have a natural destination magnet; that is, until summer's heat presses down on this treeless bench. It's so bright that I have to adjust cap and sunglasses; given the oppressive heat, I wonder if I've brought enough water. Only two cars sit baking in the sun—refreshing after fighting the hordes falling over each other up at Jackson and Jenny Lakes. Suddenly there's a spring to my step.

The trail heads due west for two-tenths of a mile, and then begins a long eyebrow arch to the northwest, and Taggart Lake, for just shy of two miles. Even with modest elevation gain I'm sweating like a pig. This rough-and-tumble dusty trail seems to reflect radiation like a mirror. Yet,

6,000 feet higher, glaciers claim shaded cubbyholes on Teton peaks. Almost desertlike conditions explain why only two other cars wait in the parking lot.

Searching for a distraction from the heat, I'm noticing how rapidly plants are reclaiming this burn. Lodgepole pines are already established and soaking up the sun, adding another six to twelve inches of growth, perhaps more, as the season unfolds. Myriad wildflowers poke their heads out from under downed tree trunks burnt to the core. Entire microcosms flourish along rock gardens lining Taggart Creek as it splashes out of reach south of the trail—so close, yet so far away.

Another quarter-mile of walking and a trail junction appears. Right goes almost a mile to Bradley Lake; left heads to Taggart Lake a half-mile away. Planning on completing a full circuit, I'll go clockwise up to Taggart Lake and then return using the path to the right. For now, I've got incoming to cope with—a thirty-something couple literally bounding down the trail with a look of utter surprise, eyes as big as saucers and jabbering a mile a minute.

"Hey, better turn back because there's a gigantic bear feeding real close to Taggart's outlet!" the man cautions me.

She adds an exclamation to underscore just how big this bear is: "We think it might be a grizzly, it's so enormous! We're headed back to tell the ranger so that she can close this trail."

He slightly downplays the prospects of a grizzly, noting, "It's probably just a black bear, but without a doubt it's the *mother* of all black bears."

Well, it's about time the furry kind and I intersected! Seeking a better reading on what lies ahead, I ask about whether the bear has a hump at its shoulders or a dish-shaped face. He thinks it has a hump; she's certain the face isn't dish-shaped. Almost in unison they ask, "Why?"

Their question assures me that they probably don't have a reliable reading on this bear. An effective way to differentiate a grizzly bear from a black bear is through physical characteristics associated with the face and shoulders. A grizzly bear usually has a prominent hump at its shoulders—a huge mass of muscle—and a dish-shaped or concave face.

Under these circumstances it's best to assume nothing. They're on a mission and eager to get going. They can't fathom why anyone would consider going on when a bear lurks ahead. To calm them a bit, I confidently point to bear spray dangling from my pack and unclip it to make them feel better.

"You're crazy to go up there . . ." they call to me as they continue to dash on down the trail, their hands gesticulating wildly. Falling over themselves, their heads wag like bobblehead dolls on the dashboard of a stiffly sprung lowrider.

Once they turn their backs I spin and dash madly up the trail at double time, hoping the errant bruin hasn't gone up into the forest. The situation is pretty delicate and anyone in this situation should exercise extreme caution to avoid an adverse encounter. It's probably a black bear rather than a grizzly, but you just never know. I don't want to run around a curve in the trail and surprise a grizzly bear—or a black bear for that matter—even with pepper spray in hand. Pepper spray isn't foolproof, and I don't want to play the idiot in this case. Thinking rather than reacting, I cut back on my pace a bit. I don't want to turn a corner of the trail and blindly happen on the jaws of death.

A black bear's diet is 85 percent vegetable matter. Here a small male is feeding on flower tops at midday.

After one hundred yards of flat-out double time, a slower pace and more oxygen to the brain brings razor-sharp clarity to my senses. It's as though exiting from a chrysalis. My nose is sniffing for a musty scent, ears straining to hear and interpret the slightest sounds, and tongue struggling to get past the bitter-metallic taste of adrenaline to buttress my early-warning system. However, it's my eyesight that magnifies and startles with clarity and depth. I'm scanning the hillsides and little ravines, looking for any movement as well as strange-looking brown or black bumps.

There's only a half-mile from the trail junction to Taggart Lake, and I must have covered half of it. As the trail rounds a bend I search a maze of old snags, vibrant three- to five-foot-high lodgepole pines, and lushly green shrubs. And then I see him.

In the distance I spy the north end of a southbound black bear skittering over a ridge. It's the most fleeting of glimpses, but the 1940 Ford rear end of this bear—a radically falling curve—and lack of a shoulder hump shout *black bear*. I never see its face to achieve 100 percent confirmation, but in my heart I know it isn't a grizzly. Finally, mission accomplished.

The bear is moving too fast. I'll never catch up as it disappears from sight. So, I go back to a pedestrian pace. Pounding heart and gushing pulse tone down. Senses return to a nonacute level. I'm left alone with the sighing of wind gradually rushing over the hillside, spalike warmth swirling around me, a riotous mosaic of lavender, red, and mango flowers reaching for the sky from green ottoman clumps, and spikes of short emerald trees interspersed with rough black snags. The magic of wildness seems to evaporate around me. Or, does it?

I finish the 200-foot climb to magnificent Taggart Lake. What a beauty. It's one of those rare lakes that seem to inhabit two different ecozones. On its western side Taggart Lake hugs broodingly dense forest; black-green firs and pines shout about perpetual moisture flowing off Avalanche Canyon and Taggart Creek. Meanwhile, to the east Taggart Lake opens to big sky left in the wake of an intensely hot forest fire. Sun smothers the mountainside bereft of trees large enough to battle off waves of luminous light.

Perched on a rounded granite boulder with waves gently lapping ashore, it's time to relax and enjoy this preciously wild lake. No one else is in sight. The bear has left Taggart Lake to me alone. Sun penetrates the shoulders of my flannel shirt like a heat lamp gone bonkers. Zephyrs float past, stirring tree limbs and branches while waving a merry salute to summer. For several minutes I just sit still and blend with this glorious setting.

A line of sawtooth spires dances north, still encrusted in snow and ice. Exum mountain guides are gingerly leading clients across rugged rock faces and around super-slick glaciers, seeking victory on Teton's highest pinnacles. East on the Snake River rafters whoop it up when they round a bend and drop over a set of rumbling riffles, spray washing over them. South down at Jackson Hole weary shoppers finally give in to hunger's demands by breaking for a bit of Bubba's Barbeque. Another captivating summer unfolds in a spellbinding land.

What's so remarkable to me is how gratifying this moment has been in what many would consider a boring part of the park. Flicking a fly away from my knee, gazing on miniscule waves lapping at Lake Taggart's shore, and shaded from an overbearing sun, I fall under the magic spell of wildness. It's no different than when I jumped across that little stream flowing out of Arroyo Seco Canyon years ago in Los Angeles. The mystery of walking

Black bears are opportunists when it comes to diet. This large male, just recently out of hibernation, has found a great source of protein—a winter-killed whitetail deer.

in the wild cannot be denied; you never know what to expect whenever you start down backcountry trails.

The magic of the Tetons was *not* sighting a bear. Enchantment turned out to be invigorating encounters with mean-spirited, as well as nonchalant, moose; languid cascades sparkling over granite boulders; and hilarious moments floating the Snake. Having finally seen a bear in the Grand Tetons, my triumph seems surprisingly hollow in comparison with the rocking bounce of raft on shining water, a sparkling lake forgotten for the season, or an osprey's iron grasp of fish dinner for the young ones.

Make no mistake about it—it's always energizing whenever a bear crosses my path, regardless of whether it is black bear or grizzly. However, perhaps I've confused the means with the ends and should reappraise what it means to visit wild backcountry. Sitting quietly on Lake Taggart's shore, this recognition takes my breath away. Sighting a bear is fantastic, but it carries more robust connotations than just an intersection with what amounts to full-figured wildlife. Bears have become a metaphor for simply enjoying the sparkling wonder of wildness—the personification of what it means to walk gracefully and adventurously across untrammeled lands.

10 ⤳

BEARS, HUMANS, AND
THE SPIRIT OF PLACE

In midsummer of 2005, a 150-pound black bear sow became a little too comfortable with the alluring largesse left unguarded by careless nature lovers in bird feeders and dog dishes east of Albuquerque. Despite winter's abundant snowfall and an abnormally cool, wet spring, summer was a scorcher and uncharacteristically precipitation free. These conditions may have stunted forage in surrounding wilderness areas, thereby enticing this bear to seek easier pickings. Or, she may simply have learned from her mother how to score a quick bite to eat. Whatever the reasons, this sow soon earned an unfortunate reputation that spiraled inevitably toward human intervention.

Originally, this black bear called the Sandia Mountains home. Rising to 11,000 feet, the wilderness offers habitat for deer, cougars, bears, and desert sheep. However, these wildlands are sandwiched between city to the west and rolling piñon hills—now suburbanized—to the east. When summer monsoons and winter snows grace the land, wildlife thrives in the high mountains. But whenever food sources are marginalized, animals seek sustenance outside wilderness boundaries. These are precisely the same places where thousands of inhabitants have built homes in their efforts to psychologically escape Albuquerque.

Ever adaptable and highly intelligent, black bears are renowned for devising clever ways to fill their bottomless bellies. Instead of running

Wildlife creatures, such as deer, are in tune with their surroundings. They have a great sense of smell, good eyesight, and great hearing. By quietly observing the deer you may be surprised at what else you may see!

down to the corner market to grab a bite to eat, brazen bruins discover that people look out for their welfare in very generous ways. Or, so it must seem from a bear's perspective. Why go to all that trouble of traipsing up and down a mountainside in search of food? Everything needed to slake a hungry bear's appetite is readily available in curious, clear-plastic cylinders hanging precariously from tree limbs, or in stainless-steel dishes reeking a bit too much of noisome canines.

Just because people love to live in wildlands and forests doesn't mean that they synchronize their beliefs and actions accordingly. More often than not, transplanted urbanites fail to understand that their lovely homes intrude on the livelihood of animal friends. Exurbanites want to be surrounded by nature, but not too close to it. Wildlife is welcome so long as it maintains a respectable distance. Cougars, bears, and bobcats that might hurt them or their pets are absolutely verboten. It's selective nature these latter-day mountain dwellers seek.

Unfortunately, no one explained this to our 150-pound sow with the light-brown muzzle. The reality she knew was an incredible bounty waiting in people's backyards. Intending no harm, she responded naturally to the tantalizing cafeteria people thoughtlessly left outside. Fantastic combinations of birdseed sat there for the taking—gray-black sunflower seeds, thistle, buckwheat, rice, flax, rape, corn, and milo were her stock in trade. Real treats occasionally cropped up—peanut butter or peanuts, orange halves, suet, raisins, and even potatoes. So little time, so many choices. To wash it all down her favorite drink was a sweet red liquid concoction—difficult to access through an array of tiny holes in hummingbird feeders. And the cost? Several times she was dive-bombed by audacious hummingbirds, barked at by frightened dogs, or accosted by irate people. These were trivial prices to pay.

That is, until authorities were notified.

On June 28, 2005, she suffered the indignity of being shot in the rear end with a dart. The next thing our sow knew, she was in a narrow, corrugated-metal tube being shipped seventy miles to the west and released somewhere on 11,000-foot Mount Taylor. Surely this distance would put an end to her marauding forays. Order returned to the East Mountains—for a short time.

Four days later, on July 2, the sow had made it halfway back to her home in the East Mountains. She was first spotted on the western outskirts of Albuquerque and chased up a tall, wooden power-line transmission pole. Game and Fish authorities moved in with a trap to capture her, but somehow she eluded them, vanishing into the night. The ghost bear would not remain under the radar for very long.

Eight days later, on July 10, our black bear was found on the edge of Moriarty—a rapidly growing town in the East Mountains. Somehow this sow managed to work her way through or around three-quarters of a million people living smack-dab in the middle of her path, across two major interstates (I-25 and I-40), and over roughly thirty-five miles since last being hung up on the power-line pole. A green plastic tag stapled to her ear helped Game and Fish officers identify her as the wandering bear. She was discovered running through yards and scaring livestock, so, for the second time, she was shot with a tranquilizer and a green tag was added to the remaining free ear.

This time Game and Fish was determined to put an end to the matter. They hauled her northwest almost one hundred miles beyond Cuba, New Mexico, and the terminus of the San Pedro Parks Wilderness. This essentially places the entire Jemez Mountain range between her and her "home," as well as vast acres of high desert wilderness relatively free from human encroachment. What finer country could a bear ask for, given the lush, parklike meadows dotted with spruce and aspen groves? Enchanting streams wend their way down through crystal-clear mountain air at ten thousand feet. It's Shangri-la for any bruin—except for this obstinate sow.

On July 25, a Monday, our black bear is located in a town park just before dawn —*one hundred miles under her paws in reaching home turf*—enjoying a wonderful garbage breakfast. It's the last straw for Game and Fish. They tranquilized her and sentenced the sow to death, in keeping with their "three-strikes" policy.

For the majority of New Mexicans, it's a funny story about a bear's tenacity and cunning in eluding Game and Fish officers. Others breathe a sigh of relief since the nuisance bear is just a memory: Now Fifi and Rover can roam free in their backyards. There will be no more messes to clean up from spilled bird food. Mountain suburbia creeps one step closer to emulating metropolitan Albuquerque.

This black bear's determination to return home is admirable, even legendary, but it overshadows a question many New Mexicans should have pondered. How did the bear know her way home? Despite being transported seventy miles in one case and one hundred miles in another—in unknown terrain—she was still able to safely negotiate her way back home. How many people could have done the same if plopped down into an unknown location far from their homes?

Scientific and popular literature describe a strong "homing instinct" or "homing behavior" on the part of bears that is similar to pigeons and other mammals. Yet, this capacity is not well understood. Some attribute it to an ability to read the position of the sun, stars, or moon. Others hypothesize the ability to sense magnetic fields. In fact, we just don't know exactly how bears (and many other mammals) are able to find their way back home after being relocated.

A potentially dangerous situation, in fact doubly so because this bear has found a winter-kill elk carcass and because she has a spring cub hidden nearby. It pays to be very alert when hiking in the woods in early spring!

A friend of Apache descent offered a plausible explanation. He told me that when he was young, his mother repeatedly instructed him to lie down and embrace the Earth. She explained that this loving contact would help him come to know the spirit of their home. It would provide a *spiritual compass*, and he would never become lost if he nurtured this awareness.

He went on to say that animals have always remained attuned to the spiritual character of their home. It helps them navigate in this confusing world. Our black bear sow lived a life connected to the spirit of her home. She was able to find her way back to where this spiritual connection was exceptionally vibrant. This feat is hardly limited to black bears. In the same manner, curlews leave Alaska in late August and fly nonstop 5,000 miles across the Pacific archipelagos to Tahiti and other islands. Like our friend the bear, they have cultivated a spiritual compass focused on home.

More questions than answers remain about the spirit of place and how animals develop this homing instinct. For example, how does a snow goose raised on the arctic tundra during summer know where to migrate to in fall? Is the spirit of place encoded in DNA? Do the young simply follow their parents and fellow birds? While scientists figure out answers to these questions, we remain awestruck by the adventures of our black bear and other animals.

Perhaps we need to listen more closely to wise people like my friend who urge us to embrace the Earth. But our hearing is so limited. There is so much competing for our attention—new tunes on our satellite car radios, a repository of favorite songs on our iPods, fashionable clothes, cars, and homes, an expanding array of electronic entertainment, and so forth. So we tend to ignore the obvious while the comforts of civilization essentially erode our capacity to recognize the spirit of place. Thus disconnected, any old place will do to lay our heads or build our homes.

There was a time when our ancestors shared in the black bear's little secret. They too knew the spirit of their home, their place on Earth. Echoes of this knowledge still resonate today.

The Land of Enchantment—New Mexico—is renowned for its remarkable spirit of place, especially the central mountain corridor running from Santa Fe to Taos. Some believe that these mountains—the Sangre de Cristo, or Blood of Christ—are distinctive power vortices. As a result people possessing diverse spiritual beliefs flock to New Mexico, including New Age, Baha'i, Shamanic, Christian fundamentalists, Tibetan Buddhist, Sufi, Roman Catholic, and other groups that sense a deep soulful connection between place and their faith. Some maintain that the high deserts and canyon country nurture sacred centers, hallowed sites worshiped by ancient people and present-day Puebloans.

Located at the intersection of remarkable natural features—stratospheric peaks, the life-giving Rio Grande, and high, sage-covered desert, Taos and Santa Fe have attracted international attention as destination magnets. Folks come from all over the globe for an intoxicating pastiche of exotic experiences, sights, scents, and flavors. Most are totally captivated by the cowboy-meets-Indian decor, the elegant magnificence of adobe architecture, and bohemian community. However, they usually fail to scratch past the surface—the pretty people, natural scenery, and inspired art.

Outside Santa Fe, a popular trail snakes its way to Nambe Lake in the Pecos Wilderness. Morning's lingering crispness reflects the signature of the Sangre de Cristos. Hidden in shade from solemn fir sentinels, it's time to take a breather and let a smidgen of doubt fully simmer in my fuzzy mind. Will I ever see this unforgivable hillside's crest or the sparkling gem waiting in Lake Peak's basin, high above the Rio Grande?

Pausing on this mountain's vertical rocky flanks, I wait until equilibrium returns; remnants of frigid night air envelop my perspiring body. Frosty conditions speak blatantly about altitude and dominating peaks thrust almost two miles into cobalt-blue sky. Gasping in the oxygen-deprived atmosphere and bent over with hands on knees, there's plenty of time to do a close-order inspection of this obscure beaten path of musty woodland loam, protruding mossy rocks and roots, damp fir needles, and assorted twigs and branches. Virgin forest always offers such a miraculously fascinating mosaic of life and organic material.

As my breathing settles, a raft of questions begins popping up. I live at 6,000 feet; what must those poor schlubs who are visiting from the heartland feel when they finally hike Pecos trails? Is this self-imposed torture really necessary? Hasn't the real victory already been won? Having labored this far, isn't the final half-mile to Nambe Lake merely an academic matter? Chest heaving from oxygen deprivation, forces conspire to end it all right there and return down, gloriously down, to the warmth of brilliant yellow sunlight where Winsor Trail crosses Nambe Creek.

Bands of light filter through black stunted fir trees twenty yards above. It's only a few minutes at most until Nambe Lake Trail levels out along the sunlit creek. Burbling waters beckon, calling from rocky channels in the plunging ravine. They're mocking anyone who stops short of the waiting alpine cirque. Determination raises its ugly head and argues persuasively against quitting with the destination so near at hand. But, it's the promise of warming chilled bones that finally clarifies my decision and causes each boot to be gradually lifted as I pick up the pace.

On topping the rise a mesmerizing flood of sublime light washes over the forest, creating a spectacle that is otherworldly. The path gently brushes streamside amidst sparkling towers that moments earlier were dark-green brooding spruces. Golden radiance infuses the hillside. Inexplicably the world seems surreal—so pristine and unbelievably perfect. A clump of delicate lavender columbine springs confidently from a chaotic jumble of granite rocks. Gray-green moss serves as perfect background and counterpoint to a profusion of vivid flowers—white yarrow, purple harebell, dew-laden bluebonnets, and red paintbrush. Achingly clear, Nambe Creek splashes noisily down the rocky ravine with great gusto, frothing and tumbling on its trip to lower elevations and eventually toward the Rio Grande.

Who wouldn't be entranced by this beauty—this combination of sunlight, creek, rockfall, firs, moss, flowers, peaks, and sky? Mostly I am struck dead center by the light of wonder—that occasionally we're privileged to witness such splendor; beauty beyond human design, fabrication, or understanding. Looking upslope, only a wave of mellow, infusing light is visible to soften the wildness. With crystal clarity I now know why I, like so many others, seek solace in wild places. And, without any effort, I fully understand the supreme spirit of place radiating from these Sangre de Cristo peaks.

How many before me have been stopped dead in their tracks like I am right now—anchored in place by something so much larger than life? Long before the Spanish conquistadores staked their claim to these mountains, Indians lived in harmony with the land. Undoubtedly they were also drawn to Nambe Lake in the course of hunting, gathering edibles, and seeking spiritual succor. When summer's intensity along dusty Rio Grande canyon lands went unabated for weeks at a time, did some follow faint paths up the Rio Nambe to its source?

It's easy to visualize a steady stream of humanity over the eons weaving among the aspens and fir, and scaling perilously vertical hillsides, in order to reach a special sanctuary in a hidden alpine bowl. Pre-Puebloan tribes were followed by ancestral Indian communities along the Rio Grande's length, and spread throughout the Four Corners. How many

Bears inhabit some of the most scenic areas North America.

tribal members over the centuries reached Nambe Lake and scores of similar subalpine and alpine lakes in the Sangre de Cristo Mountains? Did descendants of the conquistadores follow the same paths, chasing directions handed down in folklore to rediscover this jewel tucked away above the tree line?

Even as a path was progressively beaten through meadow grasses by bare feet, moccasins, leather shoes, and finally, high-tech hiking boots, did each subsequent visitor still feel the thrill of isolation? As they plodded up the mountainside with sweat dripping from their brows, did it occur to them that not many had gone this way before? Above all, did they sense the special qualities of Nambe Lake and its unfathomable history, where the spirits of ancestors still held reign?

Breathing and fascination quelled, it's time to push on. The remainder of my trip unfolds pleasantly enough. First, there is a long walk through a lush, bright-green meadow dotted with showy granite boulders, spindly spruce trees, and hillocks of jade grasses waving delicately in an almost imperceptible breeze that flows down from Lake Peak, towering above at 12,000 feet. This meadow once lived as a lake before being transformed over the years by erosion of the very mountain that gave it life. Inexorably, sedimentation completed the job. At the meadow's far eastern end, the trail I'm following crosses over Nambe Creek, released from incarceration in an alpine tarn two hundred feet or so above.

Winding through dense forest on increasingly rocky tread, I'm searching for the lake that hunkers down in a wintry basin of rock and earth. Billowing clouds of breath attest to glacial conditions this lake endures for much of the year. Up here at 11,700 feet, it takes some time to heat this bowl of trapped alpine air. Meanwhile, Nambe Lake waits patiently to sparkle in the rising sun and dance with merry waves when summer zephyrs blow across its glossy face.

It's hard to imagine anyone failing to register the extraordinary character of this lake, especially after investing all of the effort needed to reach it. Even young folk leave the dark forest shouting, "Wow, look at that!" and "Hey, cool," or "Are there fish in there?" before rushing headlong to the glistening waters. Some might argue that kids aren't really fascinated by Nambe Lake's soul. Like kids anywhere, they just see it as a unique playground. But I beg to differ. Nambe Lake radiates an obvious spirit that even young people tune in to. However, younger (and older) folk generally do not remain fixated on the lake's spirit because they have more important things to do—rocks to toss in the water, shoes to get wet, and dragonflies to chase.

The trail weaves out of forest to the outlet stream on Nambe Lake's northern shore. Suddenly the world opens up and for a brief second, I'm transported back to that moment of wonder lower on the mountainside when I was bathed in a unique spell of the right light, the right temperature, the right shadow, the right vegetation, and the right spirit. I've befriended many lakes in the Rockies, Appalachians, Cascades, and Sierras, but none have insisted that visitors linger quite like this tarn.

For a moment it's time to just sit in the warming sun while thinking of nothing; absolutely nothing at all. Cold air still hangs heavy over the lake, but a dark fleece shirt is soaking up rays like a blotter; there is satisfaction in knowing I picked the right color to wear today. At these elevations, even in midday, a little shot of warmth is welcomed when breezes begin to swirl. Hot and cold play tag around me while this rocky cauldron springs to life.

I'm perched on a flat, picnic table–sized granite boulder etched by black lichen overlooking the lake. Perhaps a couple acres in size and only a few feet deep, it's shaped like a hot-air balloon. Sun twinkles off Nambe Lake's ever-so-slightly rippling surface, causing me to squint. I gradually just close my eyes while this rocky basin's beauty locks into memory. Actually, it's a good excuse to teeter toward a nap; however, I'm content to simply just sit there and let this place gradually enfold me.

Most people seldom stop to think about how aggressively they intrude on a special spot such as this. Fixated on reaching a goal, they come marching up the trail with all sorts of bluster and fanfare, insensitive to what life in the rocky basin might feel. Now that I've settled into the lake's setting, life returns to normal. Merely sitting there motionless enables me to become part of the web of life. A fly comes buzzing over to visit, drawn by an elixir of scent evaporating off my clothing. It's content to sample a few patches of skin on my neck and wrist until it gets a whiff of the open pack; there's food in there somewhere, and this fly is intent on claiming an unanticipated gift.

My footfalls having dissipated and hurricane breathing fallen to a sigh, a persistent trickle of water can be heard to the south—springs replenishing the lake. This delicate water music is like a set of gentle chimes continuously playing an Aeolian melody with

Part of the fun of hiking in bear country is the fantastic scenery. Most of the time you will be very lucky to catch even a glimpse of a bear—so enjoy whatever nature offers.

new chords randomly thrown in every thirty seconds or so. A brief bout of wind sings harmony among the firs lining the northern shore, while waves lapping on rock drum counterpoint. The spirit of Nambe Lake, set to music.

The lake's mood shifts in and out as wind, sun, and cloud continuously rearrange themselves as if in a chaotic opera. What a sweet destination this has been. However, I'm unable to keep my thoughts empty now that a bit of cloud overhead has entered the picture. I still have to hike back to the car, and one option is to scale steep scree banks to the south a hundred feet straight up and then descend ski runs to the waiting car. This will cut off a bit of mileage, but more importantly, it provides an incentive to climb Lake Peak and reap fantastic vistas that only a 12,000-foot peak can deliver.

Joints creaking and stiff muscles complaining about further exertion, I carefully balance from one boulder to another until I reach an avalanche chute among copses of fir. From here it's straight up with no turning back; just kicking my boots into soft, needle-covered dirt, trying to keep from slipping down two steps for every step upward. One hundred feet later and almost on Lake Peak's alpine ridge, I stop for a breather, spinning around to look back down on the lake while clutching several roots for dear life.

While hanging there like a telephone lineman fixated on an intricate repair, it suddenly occurs to me that others have probably taken this shortcut in their zeal to go home. The chute offers an invitingly natural route to Lake Peak's ridge. Is this another ancient path? Call me paranoid, but I swear that I'm not alone. The sensation is difficult to put into words; it's akin to being with four or five friends at a favorite restaurant, except they're not physically present, and I can't seem to cross the veil that hangs between us.

Below me the bright button of Nambe Lake reposes in tranquility. From this vantage point I'm able to capture its scenic beauty, but I'm still too far away to be bathed in its spirit. For many, Nambe Lake is just another destination, another hiking goal to tick off at home while planning for the next Pyrrhic victory. But as far as I'm concerned, the lake represents a metaphor for the soul of these mountains.

I'm doing more than hugging some gnarly roots, spindly saplings, and sap-covered fir branches. Similar to my Apache friend, I'm literally reaching out and embracing the Earth, feeling its pulse and becoming one with its rhythm. And as I swivel and pull my way up another fifty feet to reach the ridgeline, it occurs to me that I'm also leaving a bit of my spirit behind that others may detect when they follow this obscure, but well-used, path.

In more ways than not, the black bear sow and I both shared a unique sense of spirit found along the mountainous reaches of New Mexico. Our experiences were far beyond merely enjoying some marvelously scenic country, although the picturesque nature of this land cannot be denied. *What differentiates this beautiful place is its soul, its spirit.* It's the same spirit that guided our bear—a single short life dedicated to embracing the land. It's the same spirit that my Native friend was instructed to hold onto as a way to know his home, Mother Earth. It's equivalent to the tangible spirit I felt about a diminutive little tarn outside historic Santa Fe.

Bear and human became one—the unlikeliest duo of souls journeying through life in their separate, yet indistinguishable, ways. Sadly, our black bear sow was the most proficient of the two in knowing and remaining true to her spirit of place. She pursued it relentlessly until her final day.

Although the bear was fortunate to reach her epiphany in a truly distinctive land, many other places around the world are recognized and celebrated for their unique spirits. In this respect, Taos and Santa Fe are not exclusively better than these other places. In fact, June 2005 also proved to be a fatal month for a young grizzly male in the forest surrounding Canmore, Alberta, the gateway to internationally acclaimed Banff National Park, a World Heritage Site. The parallels between bears are startling despite 1,600-plus miles' distance.

Canmore in the Northern Rockies and Santa Fe/Albuquerque anchoring the southern terminus share one indisputable fact: They are surrounded by millions of acres of drop-dead beautiful wilderness. Each wears a one-of-a-kind mantle. Northern forests are nourished by longer

Bears take enormous pleasure in water. On hot summer days it is not uncommon to see them soaking, splashing, and playing.

and colder winters with higher precipitation, resulting in vast tracts of Engelmann spruce, lodgepole pine, and subalpine fir rising to stark alpine regions. Above all, the blue Canadian Rockies shine due to expansive layers of Burgess Shale. The Southern Rockies are equally majestic in terms of impressive alpine heights; however, they flow into high deserts unlike the montane forests and grasslands of their northern counterparts. Piñon pine, juniper, and sage dominate high desert landscapes.

Among the calico ecoregions surrounding Canmore and Santa Fe/Albuquerque wildlife thrives. Although grizzlies were extirpated decades ago in New Mexico, they continue to hold on precariously in Banff National Park. As with so many pristinely attractive locations, population growth has been unrelenting in Canmore. Second homes, golf courses, commercial development, and recreation presses down upon the Park's boundaries. Just like Santa Fe's/Albuquerque's oppressive appetite for wildland, Canmore devours important tracts and corridors, hindering wildlife movement. The inevitable result is confrontation between bears and humans.

A 150-pound black bear sow is scary enough for most people; the prospect of encountering a 198-pound subadult grizzly male is another. Unfortunately for the grizzly, dubbed Bear 99, the encounters eventually turned deadly both for himself and Isabelle Dube, a thirty-something teacher and avid mountain biker. Her death is a regrettable tragedy that should not be trivialized. Nonetheless, a significant aspect of Bear 99's notoriety that meshes with his black bear cousin several days' drive to the south is an unrelenting bond to home. Both bears displayed a dogged propensity to follow this spirit of place no matter what obstacles intervened—human or otherwise.

At one time Bear 99 didn't have a name. Like many three- or four-year-old subadults, he had probably been chased off by his mother in late spring and left to fend for himself. Lost and all alone on the eastern slopes of the Rockies, his dilemma was very real. He had to find enough to eat, and he especially had to avoid mature males if he wanted to live to see another year. These forces conspired to push him toward grizzlies' least-favored habitat—territories that intersect with human activity and habitation. Nonetheless, these lands can offer surprising forage, particularly in the lush valley bottoms brimming with grassy meadows, berry-laden bushes, and a cafeteria of delectable rodents.

Bear 99 first landed on authorities' radar—much like his black bear sow counterpart—when in late May he decided to graze dandelion-laden roughs along the appropriately named SilverTip Golf Resort. Perhaps he read the golf course's welcoming sign and misunderstood; although he was indeed a silvertip grizzly, the resort was meant for golf, not his grazing pleasure. Residents whose homes line the golf course were simultaneously enthralled and repulsed, similar to the case of our black bear female.

People revel in the experience of encountering bears, and then immediately recoil when they comprehend the looming danger. Down in New Mexico, this love-hate relationship quickly grew to fear. Imagine the same process unfolding up north, except multiplied by several factors. This was a grizzly, not a black bear. Adding to this bear's frightening appearance was his unusually luxurious coat. Although Bear 99 weighed only about 200 pounds, his fur was inexplicably supreme. Its rich fullness made him look like a huge critter of vastly threatening proportions. An inquisitive teenager, he didn't understand that people saw him as a monstrous boar.

All of these factors contributed to the decision made by Canadian Fish and Wildlife officers, to remove this intimidating bear before someone was seriously hurt. A cold, steel barrel trap was set and he walked right

Alaskan brown bears are quite social and it is not uncommon to see younger males play fighting.

into what must have seemed like a long, strange trip. Similar to our black bear sow, Bear 99 was rudely darted; unlike the black bear, Bear 99 was also outfitted with a GPS collar, and then transported away from possible encroachment on civilized areas and imminent intersection with vulnerable humans. However, this is the pivotal point where these stories of the grizzly and black bear diverge.

Unlike New Mexico's sow that was transported seventy miles to begin her first relocation, Fish and Wildlife had to carefully assess where to plop this endangered grizzly. Place him in another male's territory and that would only lead to the death of a precious grizzly—a stunningly beautiful one at that. A fully grown adult male would most likely attack and kill any smaller subadult male like Bear 99. New Mexico did not have to contend with this issue because a run-of-the-mill black bear sow is all too expendable. Authorities decided to place Bear 99 at the far end of his home range, nine miles to the northeast of SilverTip Golf Resort and the bustling confines of Canmore, with its congested recreational trails and green belts.

Knowing that the tenacity of New Mexico's black bear sow allowed her to find her way home over one hundred miles of uncharted wilderness, it makes sense that a clever grizzly male would also return home. Fish and Wildlife released the grizzly on May 28, and by May 29, Bear 99 had ambled seven miles from the relatively barren high country down to greener pastures and promising forage around Lake Minnewanka. He was traveling just a few miles east of Canadian Highway 1, the main thoroughfare through these mountains, and passing periodically among heavily used recreational areas, trailheads, trails, campgrounds, and boat launches.

Seven days after being relocated, Bear 99 was near the proximity of SilverTip Golf Resort, and the rest of the story that fascinates people begins to unfold. Most would rather hear about the confrontation that ultimately resulted in one person's death and Bear 99 being put down. However, even as Canadians sensationalized this confrontation and branded this grizzly a rogue killer, it remained clear that he was simply headed to a special place. Perhaps it was succulent dandelions, grass, and other forage he found close to Canmore that drove his homing instinct. Young, impetuous, and alone, maybe the human activity surrounding Canmore piqued his curiosity and filled a void after being kicked out by his mother.

Whatever the explanation that drove their homing instincts, it is clear that both Bear 99 and the black bear sow returned to places they viewed as special habitat. Both apparently felt comfortable being around humans while learning how to forage and browse within close proximity to houses, dogs, recreational areas, motor vehicles, and the most curious discovery of all, people. If even for a moment in their brief lives, black bear and grizzly doggedly pursued a lingering spirit of place—their homes.

What does it mean to live a life guided by a detectable spirit of place even though we may be blissfully unaware of the indwelling energy? Every place possesses a special spirit. It's merely a matter of being attentive to its presence and its impact on our lives. In this respect, we can do a better job of understanding how this spiritual quality affects us, our friends, our towns, and our wildlife. Such insight can help people transcend the very forces conspiring to make the wonderful gift of life benign and boring.

Global economics, fashion trends, corporate imperatives, and other oppressive forces have a tendency to drive societies toward homogeneity and *away from a distinctive spirit of place*. Is this the future that we really want? Where everything is prepackaged, Wal-Marted, and Mc-Donaldized? Some would answer affirmatively. However, deep in their hearts, many see this as a fairly grim prospect. There's hope, however. People aren't so far gone that they can't learn from an innocent black bear sow or intrepid subadult grizzly fresh out on his own.

The sow knew the wonder of a lovely home—a place on this planet that defined who she was. The grizzly had found a place that filled many needs, which called him even when he was rudely drugged and displaced. In this regard, these bears share a common bond with humans—with you. At some point in our lives, we come to know and treasure home, a place with a palpable spirit that draws us. We have a spiritual compass. Even though we may leave this special spot, it always calls us. It's calling right now.

EPILOGUE:
THE PRICE OF PASSION

Dwarf willows rustle restlessly in persistent breezes, muted like a thousand cymbals on Zoloft. It's perpetually windy in the Arctic National Wildlife Refuge (ANWR), the Beaufort Sea and polar ice cap hovering due north exhaling great swirls of horrific weather.

Swwwiiissshhh.

Perhaps it was an eternally long, drawn-out whisper of leaves, branches, and grasses parting abruptly as 300 pounds of blond barren ground grizzly muscled toward its target. Tufts of gossamer fur on the

Grizzly bear coat colors vary from dark brown to cream. The main thing to look for is the obvious hump above the shoulders and dish-shaped face.

great bear's back danced with the breezes. It crouched slightly, ears laid flat as it crept forward.

Thump. Thump . . . Thump. Thump. Thump . . . Thump . . .

It may have been soft padding paws on a cobblestone-encrusted sandy bank. Three yards away the Hula Hula swirls by with pristine glacial waters. Billowing clouds of sediment have recently settled after a small herd of caribou splashed haphazardly across several miles upstream.

Snniiifff . . . Snnoorrt . . . Grrrooowwwlll.

Possibly there was even less forewarning. The male grizzly's snot-laden muzzle pressed deeply into the tent's sidewall, probing for an alluring, mouthwatering scent behind the petrochemical-infused, ripstop nylon wall.

Maybe none of these subtle indications registered before grizzly-hell rained down on Kathy and Rich Huffman inside their tent on ANWR's coastal plain. The initial attack could have been masked by unparalleled stealth from a wizened seven-year-old reaching his prime.

Actual facts will forever elude us; our imaginations fill in the blanks as we try to cope with what many fear as the unthinkable: A grizzly preyed on two seasoned veterans comfortable with the Alaskan outdoors. We will never know exactly how the events transpired. However, one thing is clear: The Huffmans' ten-day-long kayaking trip came to a catastrophic end merely two days short of its goal.

Any inferences are tenuous. Only carnage remained by the time Officer Richard Holschen of the North Slope Borough Police Department—along with helicopter pilot Bob Mercier and copilot Randy Crosby of North Slope Borough Search and Rescue—dispatched the grizzly. The Huffmans' remains were tangled inextricably in their tent. Bitten and bruised gear was scattered about like flotsam from a camping nightmare. One critical piece of evidence suggests how quickly the attack occurred—Rich Huffman had released the lever action of his rifle but never chambered a round. It could have been a split second—a virtual whisper of time—that spelled the difference between life and death.

Jonathan Waterman, who covered the ANWR incident for National Geographic's October 2005 issue of *Adventure* magazine, weaves an alarming portrayal of vulnerability. He notes that after inspecting the devastation,

Alaska Department of Fish and Game biologist Dick Shideler concluded the Huffmans had selected an excellent camping site below a ten-foot bluff, chosen to conveniently fend off sweeping winds. That's exactly what weather-savvy camping veterans look for. Unfortunately, it also cut off any visual ability to detect roving bears. Even if the Huffmans weren't in their tent when the attack occurred, they probably did not see the bear until it was too late to react.

More chilling is the conclusion drawn by Officer Holschen and other investigators—that the Huffmans meticulously followed proper bear-country etiquette. They used bear-proof containers for their food. They had two cans of pepper spray in addition to their rifle. The Huffmans were wilderness-wise Alaskans from Anchorage. They knew how to travel through extremely remote and rugged wilderness, what precautions to plan for, and what survival equipment to carry. An emergency radio beacon was included in their duffel bag.

This leaves me scratching my head as I try to figure out how they could have prevented this attack. When even highly experienced and exceptionally prepared adventurers succumb to a grizzly attack, is there any hope for the rest of us? Thankfully, the answer to this question is an unequivocal "yes."

Doctors Tom Smith and Stephen Herrero, who have studied a century's worth of human-bear encounters in Alaska for the Alaska Science Center, concluded that group size is a statistically significant predictor of bear encounters. Probability of an encounter is inversely correlated with the number composing a group—the higher the number of people, the lower the probability of attack. Consequently, individuals are most at risk, followed by pairs.

This correlation between group size and bear encounters is one reason why some national parks (e.g., Banff National Park in the Paradise Valley and Moraine Lake areas) limit hiking to groups of *at least* six people. In Banff's case, hikers must proceed in a very tight group, bunched together. The theory is that tightness—no more than six feet between hikers within each group—allows sufficient space between groups for bears to evade people. Tight bunches also give bears the visual impression that they are dealing with a large mass.

More often than not a bear will know you are in the area long before you spot the animal. However, if the wind is really blowing hard then you and the bear are at a disadvantage. That's when trouble can occur. You never want to surprise a bear at close distance!

Had the Huffmans been camping with four other people, the physical presence of six humans with additional tents may have been enough to prevent the attack. Not only are more eyes and ears available to detect a bear, but the visual intensity of several tents also could have served as a deterrent to aggressive behavior. There truly is safety in numbers out in grizzly country.

The Huffmans placed themselves at elevated risk due to their small group size. This risk was further heightened by the context. ANWR isn't just any wilderness; it's a preserve where forage is challenging to find. A short growing season intensifies grizzlies' instinctive drive to locate huge quantities of food, *fast*. ANWR bears constantly search for sustenance, and are always ready to pounce on any opportunity. Two piddling kayakers make an awfully tempting target under these conditions.

Unlike brown bear cousins along the coast that feast on bountiful food sources, barren ground grizzlies are perpetually trying to scare up a meal.

When caribou herds initiate calving or roots are attainable, ANWR bears enjoy very brief periods of semiabundance. This is analogous to coastal bears luxuriating among sedge-grass estuaries and salmon-rich rivers. However, the rest of the year outside of hibernation, these bears face a despairingly tough time—that's why they're called *barren ground* grizzlies.

Another option for the Huffmans would have been a perimeter alarm or electric fence. These technologies are becoming standard issue among bear-worried adventurers. Alarm systems emit loud, screeching sirens to scare off bear invaders, and ostensibly wake slumbering campers. Electric fences send a jolt to unsuspecting bruins, driving them away from campers reposing within a secured area. Users are cautioned to remember that the barriers are continuously active—an important little fact to remember when getting up at night to answer nature's call.

Other preventive measures may also have given the Huffmans an advantage for surviving this attack. A floorless tent would have given them a better chance of escaping from an imprisoning nylon jail cell, assuming they were in the tent when the assault occurred. However, given ANWR's severe weather, this could increase the probability of hypothermia-related mortality if extraordinarily inclement conditions materialized. Alternatively, the Huffmans may have escaped if they had brought a loaded pistol of sufficient firepower that didn't need to be cocked or levered.

Kathy Huffman was a retired schoolteacher and Rick Huffman was a utilities lawyer. Their education and wilderness experience were assets when analyzing the harsh terrain they were about to cover. Their preparations for traveling in grizzly country were impeccable. Nonetheless, they met an unenviable demise. Was this simply a quirk of fate—the price to be paid for following their passion?

An answer to this question circles back to Jonathan Waterman's insightful implication about vulnerability. Despite the best of precautions, it is difficult to reduce potential mortality risk to zero in bear country. Unanticipated things happen to even the most experienced and best-prepared travelers. If people can't accept being vulnerable to potential bear assaults, then they shouldn't enter wilderness areas.

Another dangerous situation: a grizzly sow with cubs feeding on a carcass.

There's enormous value to me in knowing that when I camp out in ANWR, a possibility exists that I can become a barren ground grizzly's dinner. That's what makes ANWR special in the first place. I can carefully prepare for an ANWR trip like the Huffmans did, and in an unfortunate spot—a sheltered bluff, slight hillock, or willow copse—I could still meet a grizzly who's hungry and looking for a quick meal. My bear spray may drift with erratic wind; my gun could get hung up in its holster; or any one of a thousand other little glitches could occur.

Vulnerability is the potential price to be paid for having access to and loving wild places. If this tiny chance of becoming grizzly prey was completely removed, the inherent value of ANWR and similar wilderness areas would be immeasurably weakened.

In the same vein, there's considerable worth in knowing that when I walk along a trail in Great Smoky Mountains National Park (GSMNP), I may become black bear prey. In May 2000, Glenda Ann Bradley was killed by a black bear sow with cub near the Little River and Goshen Prong trail junction in GSMNP. She was innocently waiting for her former husband, Ralph Hill, to finish fishing. When he returned and found her daypack on the ground, Ralph also discovered a black bear with a yearling cub fiercely defending their kill. Several people throwing rocks could not dissuade the bears from continuing their grisly meal. Three hours after Ralph's discovery, rangers shot the bears.

Neither people nor bears win when these predatory incidents occur. For the victims—the Huffmans, Glenda Ann Bradley, or any other victim of a bear attack—it is a lamentable loss, and deaths that should in no way be seen as unimportant. The same goes for the bears. They're unequivocally removed from the gene pool forever.

Some defenders of wildlife suggest employing aversive conditioning to alter bear behavior—Karelian bear dogs; harassment by rifled screamers, cracker shells, and rubber slugs; or other technical means. However, it is important to remember that applying these technologies to wild animals such as bears only compromises their wildness. It may create safer bears, but there is the downside of diminishing their wildness.

Black bears, brown bears, grizzlies, and polar bears are generally tolerated and even coveted, until they turn predatory. That's when alarming howls go off for authorities to intervene. People seemingly treasure the tantalizing threat of danger so long as it doesn't result in serious injury or death. That's setting an unrealistic expectation for wild animals. Wildness

Bear viewing at its best: a couple of Alaska brown bears fishing at first light.

Sibling cubs share a tender moment while their mother is off fishing.

implies animals that are roughly aggressive, not tame or domesticated, and living freely in natural environments.

For me, the issue ultimately distills to a passion for the wild, and the price I'm willing to pay to pursue my passion. I find considerable comfort in knowing that 100 percent of the danger hasn't been removed from wilderness areas. I might die from a bear attack; I could also succumb to a rattlesnake or a puma, slip down a rocky ravine, have a tree branch fall on my head, choke on beef jerky, or any other of a million unanticipated disasters. That's the thrill of backcountry exploration. My vulnerability is exquisite. If I don't watch out for me, no one else will.

Make no mistake about it. When in the immediate presence of wild bears, my adrenaline soars to soul-invigorating levels. There's nothing quite like watching a 1,000-pound brown bear boar stroll across an estuary just fifty yards away. With or without the requisite accoutrements—rifle, bear spray, noise deterrents—the hair on my neck stands up, my pulse races, and my palms drip. The bear doesn't have to maim me or kill a companion for the event to be a lasting memory and a great story to share with friends.

Merely being in the company of wild bears is enough to deeply infuse my life with an incomprehensible richness. I don't have to see bears to enjoy them. Knowing that bears may be nearby is usually enough.

Paw prints on a muddy trail in the Teton Wilderness; massive earthen excavations at a campsite in Glacier Peak Wilderness; a stinking pile of warm bruin dung in the Appalachian Mountains; or, crossing a centuries-old grizzly bear path by Lake McDonald in the Canadian Rockies—these manifestations of bears attune my senses. It's like a recklessly fast blast down the freeway in my car to clean carbon out of its cylinders. The *experience* of being in the company of bears is simultaneously tangible and enriching once you get past the fear factor.

By becoming informed about how to walk safely in bear country and pursuing these experiences, it is possible to never see a bear and yet enjoy them at extraordinarily high levels. Perhaps it isn't the bears, or their presence, that I covet the most. Maybe my passion is purely the rejuvenated sense of being totally, undeniably, alive. Walking in the company of wild bears does that for me.

A female brown bear feeding in lush vegetation and flowers.

Admittedly, I radiate with great satisfaction after directly encountering bears regardless of the setting or species. It doesn't matter if it's just a rear-end view of a black bear at Taggart Lake in Grand Teton National Park; a full-on face-down with a grizzly at Prairie Creek in Alaska's Talkeetna Mountains; or a sow with cub brushing by me in Shenandoah National Park. Their unpredictability and my vulnerability mesh in a way that fulfills my passion for life at the jagged edge.

I hope that your wilderness wanderings are enriched by the company of bears. Take prudent precautions to minimize vulnerability, but don't let sensational stories about maulings or deaths chase you away from the backcountry. You have a higher probability of being killed while innocently driving to a trailhead, or even to the mall. And, as you walk those dim forest paths; skirt fog-shrouded mountain meadows; plunge through impenetrable copses of willow; or raft by a side stream brimming with spawning salmon, look for bears.

Wait a minute!

. . . What's that rustling through the scrub oak just ahead?